The Longing, Fiery Love of the Holy Trinity

Gift to

_____

From

_____

Date

_____

"Think of the Father as a spring of life
begetting the Son, like a river
and the Holy Ghost like a sea,
for the spring and the river and sea are all one nature.

Think of the Father as a root
and of the Son as a branch
and the Spirit as a fruit,
for the substance in these three is one.

The Father is a sun with
the Son as rays and
the Holy Ghost as heat."

Saint John Damascene
Father and Doctor of the Church † A.D. 749

THE LONGING, FIERY LOVE OF THE HOLY TRINITY

The Longing, Fiery Love of the Holy Trinity

VOLUME 5

Whispers from His Infinite Love that is Always Good and Thirsts for You

By Linda Boyle

This book suits year-round devotional prayer,
but should you wish to coordinate with the
LITURGICAL SEASONS,
consider using this volume during July,
to celebrate <u>The Longing, Fiery Love of the Holy Trinity for You</u>.
The series of <u>God's Burning Love</u>, *listed with the Liturgical*
Seasons, may be seen at the back of the book.

"The Holy Trinity," Marcantonio Raimondi, c. 1500-1527

Except where noted, Scripture verses are taken from Revised Standard Version, and Revised Standard Version Catholic Editions I and II.

ISBN #: 978-1-7346330-4-7

Printed in the United States of America
Reflections, layout, art and photography selections by Linda Boyle.
Cover and book design by Linda Boyle and Susanna Allen.
This volume and all seven volumes in this God's Burning Love Series may be obtained through Amazon Books.

GOD'S BURNING LOVE FOR EVERYONE

The series of books, God's Burning Love, has been produced with no profit to the author. They are a project born out of obedience and love for the Lord, and are offered as a means of sharing our Faith. You are invited to use the books in evangelizing others. Consider sharing the power of Scriptural Reflections in your own life by writing a review, and pray with us that others will hunger to deeply know God's love for them!

Our Prayer of Love for the Holy Trinity

SAINT CATHERINE OF SIENA, DOCTOR OF THE CHURCH, 1380

Eternal Trinity,

Godhead, mystery as deep as the sea,
You could give me no greater gift than the gift of Yourself.

For You are a fire
ever burning and never consumed which
itself consumes all the selfish love that fills my being.

Yes, You are a fire

that takes away the coldness, illuminates the mind with
Your light and causes me to know Your truth.
By this light, reflected as it were in a mirror,
I recognize that You are the highest good,
one we can neither comprehend nor fathom. And
I know that You are beauty and wisdom itself. The food of angels,

You gave Yourself to man in the fire of Your love.

You are the garment which covers our nakedness, and in our hunger
You are a satisfying food,
for You are sweetness
and in You there is no taste of bitterness,

O Triune God!

Your Name: _____   Date: _____

Preface

Know His Still Small Voice... His Whisper.

God's Beloved One,

In Kings 19:12 we read, "and after the fire a still small voice." Elijah listened for the voice of God and only then came to know God's voice as a still small voice, a whisper in the quiet. Jesus says to us in Mark 6:31, "Come away by yourselves to a secluded place, and rest awhile." And in Matthew 26:38, "Remain here, watch with Me."

Oh that we would come away to a quiet place with His burning, living heart. We are called to remain there with Him, and watch with Him, friend to friend, lover to Beloved, present to Him and with Him, a comfort to Him and He to us.

We read in Song of Songs 2:10, "My Beloved speaks to me and says to me: 'Arise, my love, my fair one, and come away." It is the desire of Jesus' heart, even now today, that we would come away with Him! There is so much noise in the world that distracts us—especially digital "noise"—but nevertheless we need to listen for God's quiet whisper. In John 10:27 Jesus says to us, "My sheep hear My voice – My sheep listen to My voice." We are His sheep and He longs for us to tune our ears to the quiet whisper of His shepherding voice.

As we read, reflect, and respond with a longing for Jesus, my prayer is that we will develop a heart that is more finely tuned in to the Father. Know that God Himself is burning with love for us, and waiting for us to know His whispering voice today. He desires that we may remember all He has said to us, and He draws us again and again and again to remain with Him. We are His Beloved One. *He knows our voice!*

This book is separated by style to promote clarity about who is speaking:
- Personal reflections in *The Longing, Fiery Love of the Holy Trinity,* are in regular print, with lines generally indented to the right.
- If personal prayers are included in the reflections they are in *italics* and generally printed in the center of the page and enclosed in light blue boxes.
- Bible Scriptures are in regular print and in quotation marks.
- If saint quotes are included with the reflections, the saint quotes are in red boxes, with the exception of saint quotes in the front section of the book and on the three section dividing pages.
- Directions for lectio and visio divina, if desired, are on a gold background.

*The goal of The Longing, Fiery Love of the Holy Trinity
is to help us to hear the whisper of God's fiery love for us
in our daily lives.*

*This book mirrors a similar format to My Other Self – the
Catholic classic that was first published in 1957– wherein
the reflections are presented in the first person of Jesus.
In the same manner Reverend Francis Martin, Doctor of
Sacred Scripture, likened this use of the first person for
God and the Mother of God, to My Imitation of Christ by
Thomas á Kempis.*

*"We confess the Father and the Son and the Holy Spirit to be consubstantial,
three hypostases, one essence, one divinity. That is the true faith which has been
handed down by the fathers."*

Saint Epiphanius † A.D. 373

Author's Note

God's Beloved One,

I invite you to read these reflections as though God is speaking personally to you! My deepest hope is that while reflecting on the Scriptures and photographs, you will be inspired to realize that God truly longs to whisper His own words to you... personally into your own longing heart. His love awaits you... and is forever leading you, that you may find Him... **drawing you through the midst of His gentle, fiery love.**

These are my reflections from different seasons of life, representing over 45 years of sensing God's quiet whispers during my own personal prayer, in times of both joy and sorrow. Through the midst of His fiery love, I sensed the whispering of God saying within, "The words in these reflections are for others as well. Know that this is not of your own heart... but of Mine. All you need do is listen to My still quiet whisperings, all you need do is write. Write that others too may know who I am... that others may know the burning of My heart for them."

In my own life early on, I was filled with need and longing for Jesus Christ, then with maturity I experienced a hunger for more of God, deeper repentance, and a further powerful outpouring of the Holy Spirit while being prayed over at a Catholic prayer service. Joy flooded my soul, along with a hunger for the beauty of God's Word in both the Old and New Covenant Scriptures. The Mass and the Sacraments came alive for me, as God led me through seasons of listening, pondering, studying Scripture, and absorbing it as a living part of my life. **How generous is Jesus' burning heart!** Through the years, with God's magnificent gift of family, my husband of almost 57 years, two sons, a daughter and eight grandchildren, came growing years of mentoring others. Being a contributing writer for "The Word Among Us," was followed by leadership in women's Bible studies and women's retreats, the joy of active parish life, couples mentoring, adoration team, and the joy of taking communion to the sick and elderly. Within all these blessings there is precious fellowship and life-long friendship. **God's faithfulness is filled with His gracious abundance, enabling me to produce these lovely full color books for evangelization, while asking for no profit. He generously too gifts His Mother to us as our own! Thus followed my deeper Consecration to the Immaculate Heart of Mary and another deeper Consecration to the Merciful Heart of Jesus. What joy!**

I mention the flow of these past events with true astonishment, overwhelming gratitude, and deep humility of heart, saying, "Who knew... who knew that God could possibly do all of this in my life?" Who now knows what the burning heart of Jesus can do in us? I find in life with the Holy Spirit a continuing surprise of transformation through the wounds of Jesus christ. Isaiah 53, verse one and six (written 700 years before Christ's passion) immediately comes to my mind. "Who - would have believed what we now report and to whom has the arm of the Lord been revealed? The punishment that brought us peace was upon him and by His wounds we are healed... We are sheep which have gone astray, each of us has turned to his own way. But the Lord has laid on Him the inequity of us all." His passionate love and power, flowing forth to us from His Cross and Resurrection, are lavish and astonishing. Be expectant! Jesus is filled with mercy and tenderness. He is longing for you, His Beloved One, to enter His heart, to be healed in His wounds, and to live a life within His burning love for you! So too does the Holy Spirit wait upon you, searching for your deep desire...always waiting for you to ask, desiring always to give you more of Himself! He desires to set your soul ablaze with longing to be one with the Father's love! Pray, "Come Holy Spirit!"

God's Beloved One,

These are just a few thoughts as you draw in closer to Jesus' gentle, fiery love.

1) **Consider keeping your own journal** while using "divine seeing," *visio divina*, and "divine hearing," *lectio divina*, on pages xxii and xxiii... giving time for Him to reveal more to you through your day. Write out golden nuggets of truth revealed in His whisperings to you... and favorite whispers of His love and mercy in prayer that you now carry with you forevermore!

2) <u>All seven devotionals in this series are individually complete</u>; book seven, <u>The Mercy Gate: Intercessions</u>, is unique in Our Lord's ardent intercession!

3) **These reflections can also be used in a parish or neighborhood small group** setting, helping to create friendship, fellowship and a real hunger for learning more of God's Word. As you are fathered in His love during the events of your day, He will often encourage you to share your spiritual gifts with others. You too will come to be astonished that His whispers bring the joy and comfort of new beginnings.

Join me in evangelizing! Gift these books to others; importantly, write a review of how through them the Lord deeply touched you, creating a hunger in other souls!

Beloved One,

I ask for your prayers as you are in mine,

Linda

Foreword

By Reverend Francis Martin

This is a beautiful collection of books! The significant turning point in every one of our lives is when we finally experience and understand the extent of the Father's love for us. The Longing, Fiery Love of the Holy Trinity and its companion volumes take us to that place of understanding, bringing us in the reflections and powerful Scriptures to the most beautiful highpoint of the past—the punch line—that Jesus died out of the Father's love for us. Pope Francis' preface in the Youcat Bible calls the Bible "a book like fire," to be read daily.[1] These reflections draw us deeper into the fire within the Scriptures. I believe that the full collection is an inspired set of books in which you will have that great experience in the Scriptures, and an opportunity to practice both *lectio divina* and *visio divina*, in much the same manner as Saint Ignatius' Spiritual Exercises, causing the beauty and the fire of the Father's love to break forth in your heart!

One of the reflections I am particularly drawn to in this collection expresses our sorrowing Father's heart. With its accompanying Scriptures and photograph, the words of Scripture plunge deep into our souls, bringing us humbly before our Heavenly Father's burning heart, and leaving us wanting to spend time with Him!

This collection of books is a poignant witness to the past writings of the truths conveyed in My Imitation of Christ, but with a current appeal that says, "come to me" through the photographs, and written in the first person with reflections short enough for people to easily absorb the truth. The highlight of this witness is Jesus speaking about the love of His Father, saying to us, "I love you as much as the Father loves Me." What does this convey? "Come to Me!" Why should I come? What have you got to offer Me? "Life!" These reflections and Scriptures offer life! The key to life is rooted in the Father's burning love. That's the heart of it. That is what drove Jesus' heart—to be with God His Father forever.

We need to ask ourselves in the morning what it means today to abide in Him. Each reflection in these volumes will lead you to know His Voice, to recognize it, and then to live your life abiding in Him whose burning love surrounds us.

---

[1] Pope Francis, Youcat Bible, Ignatius Press, Preface

Artwork on Facing Page: "The Trinity," Francesco de Mura, 1696-1782

The devil's walking stick is discouragement. Be encouraged as you ponder the beauty of these reflections, photographs and Scriptures. Come and proclaim with me, "I know where I am going. I am going to be with Jesus, and the Father forever." Come with me now to hear and to know His voice through the beauty of the words and Scriptures that are within The Longing, Fiery Love of the Holy Trinity. Come to experience and really know the fiery love of God your Father, the Holy Spirit and Jesus and His Mother.

Reverend Francis Martin, (Doctor of Sacred Scripture) Pontifical Biblical Institute:

- Founder and President of The Word Proclaimed Institute
- Professor Emeritus of The New Testament, Dominican House of Studies
- Senior Fellow at the Intercultural Forum for Faith and Culture at John Paul II Cultural Center in Washington, DC
- Chair in Biblical Studies at Sacred Heart Major Seminary, Detroit, Michigan
- Past Professor at the Gregorian University in Rome
- Past Professor at the Ecole Biblique in Jerusalem

I thank Reverend Francis Martin for this gracious Foreword.
May he rest in the peace of Christ.

Acknowledgements

Encouragement: My husband, Mike

Spiritual Direction, Prayers, Content Supervision:
Rev. John Dillon, Ph. D.

Lay Out, Photographs, Art Selection: Linda Boyle
Cover and Book Design: Linda Boyle and Susanna Allen
Technical Assistance: Susanna Allen and Emily Boyle
Visio and Lectio Divina Wording: Mary Lyn Bartek and Linda Boyle

Prayer Warriors:
Marlene and Larry Knab Family, Betty and Ken Barnes,
Sue and Joe Schuchter, Mary Ann and Bob Russo,
Aimee Natumba, Mary Ann Redden, Tish Mikan, Kathy Carmody,
Delores Hainsworth, Elizabeth Cannon, Rita Martin, Lois Jackson,
Lorrie Brescia, Laura Prizzi, Erica Deane, Janet Johnston
Dr. Thom and Carol Gardner
Mary Lyn Bartek, Karen Maxwell, Virginia Meloni
Brandt and Carol Boyle Family, Michael and Lynn Boyle Family,
Allison and Ryan Eckholm Family

Photography Credits:
Used with permission, page 87
Bruce Saunders, pages 68, 70, 104
All other images are public domain.

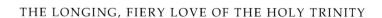

*In the gift of prayer God draws us
through His Word into His presence to rest within Him in His
Fiery Love in the Trinity. He enables, sustains and fires our desire
more and more to be one with Him... transforming us with
His Body, Blood, Soul and Divinity!
(cf. John 15.4 Passion Translation)*

"Adoration of the Trinity," Albrecht Durer, 1511

THE LONGING, FIERY LOVE OF THE HOLY TRINITY

Table of Contents

SECTION 1
God's Yearning Desire for You

SECTION 2
God's All-Seeing, All-Knowing, All-Good Love

SECTION 3
God's Infinite Design as Creator

BONUS SECTION

The Gift of Prayer

~ FROM THE CATECHISM OF THE CATHOLIC CHURCH² ~

"<u>What is prayer?</u> **Saint Teresa of Avila answers: 'Prayer in my opinion is nothing else than a close sharing between friends; it means taking time frequently to be alone with Him who we know loves us.'…Prayer seeks Him 'whom my soul loves'.** [Song of Songs 1:7] It is Jesus, and in Him, the Father. We seek Him, because to desire Him is always the beginning of love, and we seek Him in that pure faith which causes us to be born of Him and to live in Him. In this inner prayer we can still meditate, but our attention is a gaze of faith fixed on the Lord himself."

"<u>Entering into prayer </u>is like entering into the Eucharistic liturgy: we 'gather up:' the heart, recollect our whole being under the prompting of the Holy Spirit, abide in the dwelling place of the Lord which we are, awaken our faith in order to enter into the presence of Him who awaits us. We let our masks fall and turn our hearts back to the Lord who loves us, so as to hand ourselves over to Him as an offering to be purified and transformed."

"<u>The prayer of the child of God is the prayer</u> of the forgiven sinner who agrees to welcome the love by which he is loved and who wants to respond to it by loving even more. [Luke 7:36-50; 19:1-10] But he knows that the love he is returning is poured out by the Spirit in his heart, for everything is grace from God. …**Prayer is the poor and humble surrender to the loving will of the Father in ever deeper union with His Beloved Son.**"

"<u>Prayer is a gaze of faith, fixed on Jesus</u>. 'I look at Him and He looks at me': this is what a certain peasant of Ars [St. John Vianney] in the time of his holy curé use to say while praying before the tabernacle.** This focus on Jesus is a renunciation of self. His gaze purifies our heart; the light of the countenance of Jesus illumines the eyes of our heart and teaches us to see everything in the light of His truth and His compassion for all men. **Contemplation also turns its gaze on the mysteries of the life of Christ. Thus it learns the 'interior knowledge of our Lord,' the more to love Him and follow Him.**" [Saint Ignatius of Loyola]

---

² *Catechism of the Catholic Church*, Part 4 - Christian Prayer, Section 1 - Prayer in the Christian Life, Chapter 3 - The Life of Prayer, Article 1 - Expressions of Prayer, I. Vocal Prayer, paragraphs 2709, 2711-2712, and 2715, [emphasis added] [specific prayer removed]
pe

Prayer ~ Saint Teresa of Avila

"This [meditation on scripture] is the first step to be taken towards the acquisition of the virtues, and the very life of all Christians depends upon their beginning it."

"If they lose [in prayer] their Guide the good Jesus, they will be unable to find their way."

"Humans are not angels. We have bodies. We are not divine. The God-Man Jesus is our companion, our teacher [in prayer] and our nourishment in the Eucharist."

"Have an image or painting of Jesus. It is also a great help to read a little in a good book written in the vernacular in order to recollect one's thoughts."

"If a person does not think Whom he is addressing, and what he is asking for, and who it is that is asking and of Whom he is asking it, I do not consider that he is praying at all, even though he be constantly moving his lips."

"By gazing at His grandeur, we get in touch with our own lowliness… by pondering His humility, we shall see how far we are from being humble."

Introduction

Jesus invites you to Visio Divina and Lectio Divina, to encounter Him in prayer!

My Beloved (as from the voice of Jesus Christ),

My desire for you is that you would long to know more of Me, and to know more of the depth of My burning love for you. Beloved, I long for you to listen to the words personally spoken to you every day by My Heavenly Father, the Holy Spirit, and by Me. If you will only remain still and listen, then you will interiorly hear My words spoken *just to you*. I wait patiently, filled with love for you... waiting until you are near Me, that I might lavishly pour out My love upon you, My dearest one! Be drawn into My love! I ask you to quiet your heart as I lead you deeper into Mine. Be at peace within, stay still, and rest. Remember that I am here with you, in this moment and in this place. Acknowledge My presence and rest in it, asking the covering of My blood shed for you. Trust and believe that you are able to know My voice. Feel My eager anticipation, as I cannot wait to share Myself with you! Call on the Holy Spirit, and as I lead you come. Beloved, do not hesitate, jump into My love, jump into My heart! There is no need to fear, for I accept you just as you are. Come, jump into My loving, protective arms.

> ***God's Beloved, will you accept His enthusiastic invitation to jump into His arms?***
>
> *The Lord longs for this close relationship with us! He gives His Precious Blood to protect all He wishes to teach us. His heart longs for this close relationship with us. Use the "eyes of your heart" on the photographs placed with the reflections that follow, so that God might more deeply reveal Himself to you through something seen in the photographs. The visio divina of the photographs, Latin for "divine seeing," shares roots with the ancient practice of lectio divina or "divine reading" of the Word of God. In doing this Jesus desires to transform your mind and heart to prepare you for the gift of "heart" conversations with Him. After you do your "divine seeing" and "divine reading," keep your own journal, writing with Him the ways He has uniquely and individually touched your heart. Begin with a prayer. Use the following guidelines.*

Guidelines for Divine Seeing

VISIO DIVINA – "PRAYING WITH OUR EYES"
INVITES HEART PRAYER

View the chosen <u>PHOTOGRAPH</u> through your eyes and the eyes of your heart:
- Close your eyes and breathe deeply, asking for the protective covering of the precious blood of Jesus over you. Acknowledge the loving, accepting presence of the Lord with you. Ask Him to speak to you through the photograph.
- Look at the photograph presented with the reflection. What draws your attention in the photograph? Gaze upon that part for a few moments. Close your eyes still seeing the image in your mind. Rest there. Open your eyes and look at the whole photograph.
- What does the image stir up in you? What do you feel? What do you hear God whispering into your heart? What does the picture reveal to you about the Lord's heart? Consider entering into the photograph yourself. Close your eyes as you participate in the image or "become" one of the people. What do you see, sense, feel or hear? Linger in the experience.
- Rest a moment in what has been revealed. Respond to God to what is now on your heart. Take a moment to rest in God's presence.
- Jot down in your journal insights on what you found most helpful, returning to them, and Him, during your day. He goes with you!

Guidelines for Divine Reading

LECTIO DIVINA – "PRAYING WITH SCRIPTURE"
INVITES GOD TO SPEAK

Read and Reflect using the <u>REFLECTION</u> you have chosen in this book:
- First close your eyes and acknowledge the loving presence of the Lord with you. Ask for the protective covering of the Precious Blood of Jesus over you.
- Read the reflection thoughtfully, pausing to savor the word, phrases or sentences that spoke to your heart.

- What word, phrase or thought stands out to you? What is your heart drawn to? Linger here. Journal your thoughts, impressions or what the Lord discloses to you personally through the reflection.

Read and Reflect using the <u>SCRIPTURES</u> that follow the reflection you chose:
- **Read the scriptures reflectively.** Select one scripture that stands out to you and read it slowly, repeating the scripture until you quiet.
- Close your eyes and picture what the scripture looks like with the eyes of your heart, placing yourself in the picture.
- What is the picture you see? Write it down.
- As you linger in the picture what are you aware of? Be attentive to what you sense or feel coming from His heart to you personally.
- What does the scripture reveal about the heart of God?
- What does the scripture communicate to you about God's heart for you?
- Jot these things down in your journal.

Rest and be Restored:
- Relax, sit comfortably with your eyes closed and your palms up, allowing yourself to be in a posture to receive.
- With each normal in-breath, receive what has been unveiled to you.
- Soak here allowing yourself to experience His truth for you. Rest here in Him and linger in His presence.

Respond:
- Take time to talk to God about what has been revealed today and thank Him.
- He longs for these moments with you!

Remain with Him:
- He is affectionately pursuing you through the photographs, through the reflections, and through the scriptures. He is whispering to you. Know that He is walking with you, eagerly anticipating you throughout your day. Acknowledge His personal presence with you, holding in your heart what He has lovingly communicated or demonstrated to you.

God's Beloved, *visio divina* and *lectio divina* are a gift, drawing us into a longed for relationship with the burning love of the living God. We seek to know His voice for our own life, while in turn, out of His mercy, He floods our soul with His Own Spirit of Truth and Life, covering us with His wings of comfort and His delight! What a privilege He has given us, to know Him…to know His whispering voice… His burning love for us! <u>In your journal, write what the Lord has communicated to you, or draw a picture. Place this or a key phrase on a note pad, sticking it someplace close, so you will see it and ponder it throughout the day.</u>

SECTION 1

God's Yearning Desire for You

"For with Him were always present the Word and Wisdom, the Son and the Spirit, by whom and in whom, freely and spontaneously, He speaks, saying, "Let Us make man after our image and likeness;"'

Saint Ireneaus, Early Church Father † A.D. 202

"God does not change; he is Love, ever and always. In himself, he is communion, unity in Trinity, and all his words and works are directed to communion."

Pope Benedict XVI

Artwork on Facing Page: "The Holy Trinity," Peter Paul Rubens, 1577-1640

I Am Who I Am... the Trinity

Beloved, <u>look</u> at the photograph. What draws your interest? <u>Read</u> the reflection and the Scriptures, <u>reflect</u> upon them, linger, <u>rest</u> and be <u>restored</u> in My Truth. <u>Respond</u> with your heart to Me and <u>remain</u> with Me as I remain with you.

Dearest Precious Most Holy Trinity,

How is it that Your unfathomable, deep, sacrificial, humble love desires to save us with our brokenness, pride, wretchedness, and pain?
Your love so piercingly grips us with the beauty of who You are in your Triune glorious unity of being – loving us as Father, dying for us as Son... thrilling our souls as Holy Spirit, giving us hope for what is still yet to come... even in the midst of our devastation. Nothing shatters You... nothing is beyond comprehension to You.
Have mercy on us Dear God.
We are lost and we need You to find us!

Beloved,

I draw you unto Myself…
  I AM WHO I AM.
    There is no other…
      No other love… only mine that draws you.

No other Father, as I AM Father.
  No other Savior, as I AM Savior.
    No other Spirit, as I AM Spirit.
      I AM, All in All… One.
        There is no other that loves you
          As I do love you.

Know this: I AM WHO I AM… LOVES YOU!

Who is, I AM WHO I AM, you ask?

  I AM your breath and I hold you together as Father.
  I AM the True Presence and I Am always with you, as the Son… the Christ.
  I AM the Goodness that radiates between the Father and the Son as Spirit.

And We Are One in Being: Only One!

  I AM One who loves you, as a true Father, holy!
  I AM One who loves you, as a true Savior of your soul!
  I AM One who draws you to your Father and Savior in My Spirit.

And We Are One in Being: Only One!

  As One, do you not also love your little ones as a Father?
  As One, do you not also love your little ones and save them?
  As One, do you not also draw your little ones with your Spirit to Goodness?

You, My beloved, are a mere reflection of Me, created to reflect My image.

Is there not within you all three? A reflection of Me!
  Come, My Spirit, draws you to be One with Me.
    It is GOOD when you are One with Me!
      I have created you to be One with Me!
        I have loved you eternally,
          Even died for you on a "tree."
            Come, run to Me!
              Stay for all eternity…
                With Me!

Exodus 3:14, "God said to Moses, 'I AM WHO I AM.' And he said to the people of Israel, "I AM sent me to you.""

Matthew 5:45, "So that you may be sons of your Father who is in heaven; for he makes his sun rise on the evil and on the good, and sends rain on the just and on the unjust."

Hebrews 1:3, "He reflects the glory of God and bears the very stamp of his nature, upholding the universe by his word of power. When he had made purification for sins, he sat down at the right hand of the Majesty on high,"

John 14:3, 16, "And when I go and prepare a place for you, I will come again and will take you to myself, that where I am you may be also… And I will pray the Father, and he will give you another Counselor, to be with you forever,"

John 3:8, "The wind blows where it wills, and you hear the sound of it, but you do not know whence it comes or whither it goes; so it is with everyone who is born of the Spirit."

What am I personally speaking to you through the photograph, reflection and Scripture? During your day I invite you to continue in My presence, remembering those truths I have revealed to you personally, responding to Me by writing to Me what touched your heart.

"But in the one true God and Trinity it is naturally true not only that God is one but also that he is a Trinity, for the reason that the true God himself is a Trinity of Persons and one in nature. Through this natural unity the whole Father is in the Son and in the Holy Spirit, and the whole Holy Spirit, too, is in the Father and in the Son. None of these is outside any of the others; because no one of them precedes any other of them in eternity or exceeds any other in greatness, or is superior to any other in power."

The Rule of Faith 4
Early Church, A.D. 523

"Wherefore, our Lord God helping, we will undertake to render, as far as we are able, that very account which they so importunately demand: viz., that the Trinity is the one and only and true God, and also how the Father, the Son, and the Holy Spirit are rightly said, believed, understood, to be of one and the same substance or essence;"

Saint Augustine of Hippo, Church Father † A.D. 354 – 430

The Body, My Church, is Broken

Beloved,

The Body, My Church, is broken and only I can make it whole.

    Trust Me to do it. Is it too much for Me? Of course not!

        Though you might think it so! Always I have had a plan.

            Always I knew that it was coming to an end. Always I have had a plan!

New beginnings in Me…Always new beginnings…

Has it not always been…new beginnings? Nothing new on the face of the earth.

Trust in Me…in all things…even the most precious. Trust in Me!

There is nothing that does not need redemption on the face of the earth…

More than anything – the Body of My Church, the body of My Bride.

I sacrificed everything for My Bride, My Body…My Church,

As did Hosea and his bride too was a harlot!

No matter…there is nothing that cannot be washed clean.

There is nothing that cannot be made new.

There is nothing that cannot make a new beginning.

New beginnings take place at My initiative,

At My calling, at the sound and call of My voice.

Let it be so!

As My bride reels in the midst of her rebellion,

Let it be known that she is still Mine!

I will deliver her of her immorality and of her sin,

And she will sin no more in My sight as a harlot.

She will be washed whiter than snow.

It is My doing…Wait for it! Nothing is beyond My doing.

Is anything too great for Me?

Is anything beyond My scope? You know the answer!

All of creation is meant for My glory…

For out of My glory comes…

All that is good…all that is beauty!

And…the beauty of My Bride, the Church, will once again shine with radiance…

Across the face of the earth…bringing all into My sanctuary…one with Me…

And one with My Father, filled with the Holy Spirit. Wait for it!

Trust in Me to lead you…guide you…teach you. Trust in Me!

Would I leave you all alone? You are My Precious One…

Each and everyone of My children are My Precious Ones.

Each is unique…designed by Me…for My purpose…

Out of My love there is a purpose in each life…

Each life is mine…to draw unto Myself…

Into a glorious banquet of love!

Together we give glory to the Father.

Trust Me!

God's Yearning Desire for You

Psalm 104:30, "When you send forth your spirit, they are created; and you renew the face of the ground."

Hosea 14:4-9, "I will heal their disloyalty; I will love them freely for my anger has turned from them. I will be like the dew to Israel; he shall blossom like the lily...his beauty shall be like the olive tree,...They shall again live beneath my shadow, they shall flourish as a garden; they shall blossom like the vine...your faithfulness comes from me. Those who are wise understand these things; those who are discerning know them."

Proverbs 3:5-6, "Trust in the LORD with all your heart, and do not rely on your own insight. In all your ways acknowledge him, and he will make straight your paths."

Isaiah 30:15, "For thus said the Lord GOD, the Holy One of Israel: In returning and rest you shall be saved; in quietness and in trust shall be your strength."

Psalm 139:14, "I praise you, for I am fearfully and wonderfully made."

Wisdom 7:22, "For wisdom, the fashioner of all things, taught me. There is in her a spirit that is intelligent, holy, unique, manifold, subtle, mobile, clear, unpolluted, distinct, invulnerable, loving the good, keen, irresistible,"

What am I personally speaking to you through the photograph, reflection and Scripture? During your day I invite you to continue in My presence, remembering those truths I have revealed to you personally, responding to Me by writing to Me what touched your heart.

*"After Holy Communion I communed for a while with the heavenly Father.
My soul was drawn into the glowing center of love.
I understood that no exterior works could stand comparison
with the pure love of God. ...
I saw the joy of the Incarnate Word,
and I was immersed in the Divine Trinity.
When I came to myself, longing filled my soul,
and I yearned to be united with God "*

Saint Maria Faustina † 1938

THE LONGING, FIERY LOVE OF THE HOLY TRINITY

Where Is "I Am Who I Am"?
I Am All Around You

Beloved,

You see Me in the sunshine… You feel Me in the rain.
  You touch Me especially… when you reach for Me in pain…
    Though it is here… that you will find… there is much to gain.

You know that I am close in child-like laughter.
  You know that I am near in the silence of your tears.
    You smell Me in the blooming spring time…in a bride's bouquet…
      And in the sweetness of companionship… after many years!
        You hear Me in the wind that blows…
          You hear Me in a song that draws you near…

You sense Me in a baby's touch… and after many years…
Remembering that My presence too was there.

Know that I Am near you now… especially when lost … or wanting…
Know that I have been close to you always… always through the years.
Know that I know all your joys and all your sorrows…
I am the One who has held you up…and carried you along.

Soon we can be together! Prepare now for the trip!
Long have I waited for you Beloved….and there is much to come!
Yes Beloved, much to come… Together let's run!

WORD OF GOD

Genesis 27:27, "So he came near and kissed him; and he smelled the smell of his garments, and blessed him, and said, "See, the smell of my son is as the smell of a field which the LORD has blessed!"

Psalm 32:7, "Thou art a hiding place for me, thou preservest me from trouble; thou dost encompass me with deliverance."

Psalm 42:8, "By day the LORD commands his steadfast love; and at night his song is with me, a prayer to the God of my life."

2 Timothy 4:17, "But the Lord stood by me and gave me strength to proclaim the word fully, that all the Gentiles might hear it. So I was rescued from the lion's mouth."

Psalm 31:1-2, "In thee, O LORD, do I seek refuge; let me never be put to shame; in thy righteousness deliver me! Incline thy ear to me, rescue me speedily! Be thou a rock of refuge for me, a strong fortress to save me!"

What am I personally speaking to you through the photograph, reflection and Scripture? During your day I invite you to continue in My presence, remembering those truths I have revealed to you personally, responding to Me by writing to Me what touched your heart.

"Let your old age be childlike, and your childhood like old age; that is so that neither may your wisdom be with pride, nor your humility without wisdom."

Saint Augustine of Hippo † A.D. 430

Be With Me Through the Day

Beloved, <u>look</u> at the photograph. What draws your interest? <u>Read</u> the reflection and the Scriptures, <u>reflect</u> upon them, linger, <u>rest</u> and be <u>restored</u> in My Truth. <u>Respond</u> with your heart to Me and <u>remain</u> with Me as I remain with you.

Beloved,

I who am God call you by name… My own Beloved.

Beloved, begin on your knees in your heart and in your life…

Be present to Me… and there we shall begin.

Speak to Me about your day and you will then know,

Where we are to go and what we are to do.

We will do work together, you and I.

We will win souls together, you and I.

Let us begin. There will be no end…

Trust Me, I know all of your concerns.

I know all of your desires.

My desire is to give to you the deepest desires of your heart and
    I would give you more… because I know those things
        I long to teach you.
           I know the things I long to share with you and
               To experience with you,
                  Those things that will touch the hearts of others.
                     So many needing to be touched… I will take you there.
                   So that together we can touch them…
                   Together…
                   Together…
                   Together.

WORD OF GOD

Colossians 1:17, "He is before all things, and in him all things hold together."

Colossians 2:2, "That their hearts may be encouraged as they are knit together in love, to have all the riches of assured understanding and the knowledge of God's mystery, of Christ,"

Colossians 2:13, "And you, who were dead in trespasses and the uncircumcision of your flesh, God made alive together with him, having forgiven us all our trespasses,"

Colossians 3:14, "And above all these put on love, which binds everything together in perfect harmony."

What am I personally speaking to you through the photograph, reflection and Scripture? During your day I invite you to continue in My presence, remembering those truths I have revealed to you personally, responding to Me by writing to Me what touched your heart.

"Enrich your soul in the great goodness of God:
The Father is your table, the Son is your food, and the Holy Spirit waits on
you and then makes His dwelling in you."

Saint Catherine of Siena † 1380
Doctor of the Church

Have I Ever Let You Down?

Beloved, <u>look</u> at the photograph. What draws your interest? <u>Read</u> the reflection and the Scriptures, <u>reflect</u> upon them, linger, <u>rest</u> and be <u>restored</u> in My Truth. <u>Respond</u> with your heart to Me and <u>remain</u> with Me as I remain with you.

My Child,

In Me there is life and health and strength.
   All things exist in Me, for Me, and to glorify Me.
      It is I who hold the universe together.
         Be freed and know all things are possible with Me for the redeemed.
         Be at peace, I am with you. I have rescued you, My child,
            But I have not rescued you for life to be easier for you,
               But that you might know Me and love Me and serve Me.

My will and My purpose for you and your life are
   Not the same as your will and your purpose for your life.
      But from My will and My purpose come life, and from
         Your will and your purpose often come "death" and suffering.
            Seek to know Me and love Me. Seek to know and to do My will.

Do not be afraid of not being able to follow.
I will give you the strength and the ability.

Have I ever let you down? Others have let you down. Have I ever let you down?
Haven't I been faithful to you always? So too will I be faithful in this
That you find so difficult. I have planted you near streams of
Living water that gives to you hope for what is yet to come.
Hope that gave to you new beginnings, brings hope at the end!
Ever a time of surprise and unexpected conclusions…
From "your Lord", who is The master story teller…
And Creator of all.

WORD OF GOD

Baruch 3:23, 32, 35, "The story-tellers and the seekers for understanding, have not learned the way to wisdom, or given thought to her paths… But the one who knows all things knows her…This is our God; no other can be compared to him."

1 Peter 4:12, "Beloved, do not be surprised at the fiery ordeal that is taking place among you to test you, as though something strange were happening to you."

1 Peter 1:21, "Through him you have come to trust in God, who raised him from the dead and gave him glory, so that your faith and hope are set on God."

Mark 14:36, "And he said, 'Abba, Father, all things are possible to thee; remove this cup from me; yet not what I will, but what thou wilt.'"

1 Titus 1:12, "I thank him who has given me strength for this, Christ Jesus our Lord, because he judged me faithful by appointing me to his service."

What am I personally speaking to you through the photograph, reflection and Scripture?
During your day I invite you to continue in My presence, remembering those truths I have
revealed to you personally, responding to Me by writing to Me what touched your heart.

*"In so far as divine love beautifies our souls. And makes us pleasing to
His divine Majesty, it is called grace; in so far as it gives us strength to do
good, it is called charity; but when it reaches such a degree of perfection,
that it makes us not only do the good, but do so carefully, frequently and
readily, then it is called devotion."*

Saint Francis de Sales † 1622

Think Big

My Child,

Walk carefully My child…Listen…Watch.
> Nothing is impossible with Me, but you must listen carefully for
> > My direction and then Follow it!
> > > Knowing it is your Father who is watching over you…
> > > > Your loving caring Father.

Nothing is impossible in a life that is fully yielded to Me…Think Big!!
> How great and how wide and how far is My love for you…
> > How kind and how deep! Your sins are as grains of sand to Me.
> > > You are to dwell so completely aware of My love,

That My love might truly dwell in you. I love you My child!
Dwell this day in Me, know My love. Come live in Me!

Yes, Father!

WORD OF GOD

John 15:9, "As the Father has loved me, so have I loved you; abide in my love."

John 15:14, 15, "You are my friends if you do what I command you. No longer do I call you servants, for the servant does not know what his master is doing; but I have called you friends, for all that I have heard from my Father I have made known to you."

Matthew 19:26, "But Jesus looked at them and said to them, "With men this is impossible, but with God all things are possible."

Psalm 40:6-86, "Sacrifice and offering you do not desire, but you have given me an open ear. Burnt offering and sin offering you have not required. Then I said, "Here I am…I delight to do your will, O my God; your law is within my heart."

What am I personally speaking to you through the photograph, reflection and Scripture? During your day I invite you to continue in My presence, remembering those truths I have revealed to you personally, responding to Me by writing to Me what touched your heart.

"In so far as divine love beautifies our souls. And makes us pleasing to His divine Majesty, it is called grace; in so far as it gives us strength to do good, it is called charity; but when it reaches such a degree of perfection, that it makes us not only do the good, but do so carefully, frequently and readily, then it is called devotion."

Saint Francis de Sales † 1622

"God yearns to be yearned for."

Saint Gregory Nazianzen † A.D. 389

Be Assured

My Child,

Be assured that I love you,
    Be assured of My presence,
        Be assured that I have died for you,
            Be assured I have answered your prayers.

Know that I go before you.
    I am the Almighty who was, who is and who is to come.
        Behold I am the lamb of God who takes away the sins of the world.
        Behold I go before you to heal and bring home the lost.

I am with you and go before you. Do not fear, oh little one.
It is for this that you share in My sufferings. Put your trust in Me.
Know I will work this for good at the end.
I have answered the cries of your hearts....
For I am a GOOD God.

Know that all will be restored and...there will be more than before.
More love...more joy...new life...more than before.
Forever with Me...there will be more!

WORD OF GOD

Psalm 139:1, "O LORD, thou hast searched me and known me! Thou knowest when I sit down and when I rise up; thou discernest my thoughts from afar. Thou searchest out my path and my lying down, and art acquainted with all my ways. Even before a word is on my tongue, lo, O LORD, thou knowest it altogether."

1 John 5:14-15, "And this is the confidence which we have in him, that if we ask anything according to his will he hears us. And if we know that he hears us in whatever we ask, we know that we have obtained the requests made of him."

Isaiah 41:10, "Fear not, for I am with you, be not dismayed, for I am your God; I will strengthen you, I will help you, I will uphold you with my victorious right hand."

Psalm 3:2-6, "Many are saying to me, "There is no help for you in God."
But you, O LORD, are a shield around me, my glory, and the one who lifts up my head. I cry aloud to the LORD, and he answers me from his holy hill. I lie down and sleep; I wake again, for the LORD sustains me. I am not afraid..."

What am I personally speaking to you through the photograph, reflection and Scripture? During your day I invite you to continue in My presence, remembering those truths I have revealed to you personally, responding to Me by writing to Me what touched your heart.

"Thus understanding and love, that is, the knowledge of and delight in the truth, are, as it were, the two arms of the soul, with which it embraces and comprehends with all the saints the length and breath, the height and depth, that is the eternity, the love, the goodness, and the wisdom of God."

Saint Bernard of Clairvaux † 1153

Let Me Give You My Best

Beloved, <u>look</u> at the photograph. What draws your interest? <u>Read</u> the reflection and the Scriptures, <u>reflect</u> upon them, linger, <u>rest</u> and be <u>restored</u> in My Truth. <u>Respond</u> with your heart to Me and <u>remain</u> with Me as I remain with you.

My Child,

Will you lay down your life and follow Me?
    I know it is much for Me to ask, because
        It is hard for you to hear these words, but
            My child, how can My work be accomplished in and around you,
                If you are not willing to lay down your life…
                    Your desires for worldly things?
                        Can I work My desires in you and for you
                            If you still have worldly desires that you seek to fulfill?
                            Do I not know what is best for you?

Does a father give his child a snake when he asks for a loaf of bread?
    How much more then, will I not give to you…and abundantly,

    God's Yearning Desire for You

That which is good and right for you and for those you love.
Do not be afraid! Put all these things into My hands and
Let Me care for you as a loving Father. Let Me give to you My best!

Do I not know all things far exceeding what you can conceive of or dream?
Do not be afraid to suffer. Do not be afraid to experience a little bit of My Cross.
I shall make you stronger with each step, that you may in time
Carry your cross more easily and reap all of its rewards!

But you must take that first step and each step along the way.
Be willing to take the steps and I shall carry your burden.
You shall be set free, free to love…free to live out My call to you…
Free of the bondages of this world! Free to be with Me for eternity!

WORD OF GOD

Matthew 6:25, "Therefore I tell you, do not be anxious about your life, what you shall eat or what you shall drink, nor about your body, what you shall put on. Is not life more than food, and the body more than clothing?"

John 12:26, "If any one serves me, he must follow me; and where I am, there shall my servant be also; if any one serves me, the Father will honor him."

Luke 9:23-24, "And he said to all, "If any man would come after me, let him deny himself and take up his cross daily and follow me. For whoever would save his life will lose it; and whoever loses his life for my sake, he will save it."

Ephesians 4:2, "With all lowliness and meekness, with patience, forbearing one another in love.

What am I personally speaking to you through the photograph, reflection and Scripture? During your day I invite you to continue in My presence, remembering those truths I have revealed to you personally, responding to Me by writing to Me what touched your heart.

"But above all preserve peace of heart. This is more valuable than any treasure. In order to preserve it there is nothing more useful than renouncing your own will and substituting for it the will of the divine heart. In this way his will can carry out for us whatever contributes to his glory, and we will be happy to be his subjects and to trust entirely in him."

Saint Margaret Mary Alacoque † 1690

Come Away with Me

Beloved,

I sing unto you words of love and words of life.

Come away with Me My beloved, for I am yours and you are mine.

Come and spend the day with me, within your mind,

And we will share with one another words of love and words of life.

There is time…sharing words of love…and not of anxious praise.

Let us "fall in love" one with the other…

As we spend the hours communing, one with the other.

No need to rush…No need to fear…

For I will be with you… year after year, after year.

Song of Songs 2:10, "My beloved speaks and says to me: "Arise, my love, my fair one, and come away;"

Isaiah 38:20, "The LORD will save me, and we will sing to stringed instruments all the days of our life, at the house of the LORD."

1 Corinthians 14:15, "What am I to do? I will pray with the spirit and I will pray with the mind also; I will sing with the spirit and I will sing with the mind also."

Luke 12:22, "And he said to his disciples, "Therefore I tell you, do not be anxious about your life…"

1 John 4:16, "So we know and believe the love God has for us. God is love, and he who abides in love abides in God, and God abides in him."

Exodus 25:30, "And you shall set the bread of the Presence on the table before me always."

What am I personally speaking to you through the photograph, reflection and Scripture? During your day I invite you to continue in My presence, remembering those truths I have revealed to you personally, responding to Me by writing to Me what touched your heart.

*"Today I was in heaven, in spirit, and I saw
its inconceivable beauties and the happiness that awaits us after death.
I saw how all creatures give ceaseless praise and glory to God.
I saw how great is happiness in God, which spreads to all creatures making them
happy; and then all the glory and praise which springs from this happiness
returns to its source; and they enter into the depths of God, contemplating the
inner life of God, the Father, the Son, and the Holy Spirit,
whom they will never comprehend nor fathom."*

*"This source of happiness is unchanging in its essence,
but it is always new, gushing forth happiness for all creatures.
Now I understand St. Paul who said,
"Eye has not seen, not has ear heard, nor has it entered into the heart of man
what God has prepared for those who love Him"*

Saint Maria Faustina † 1938

I Am... Your God!

"The Holy Trinity," Pietro Novelli, 1603-1647

My Beloved Child,

I AM the God from whom all life does flow,

    I AM the God of all righteousness,

I AM the God who has loved you so.
I AM the God all men long to know,
I AM the God who has made you so.
I AM ... Your God, your God!

I AM the God who rose from the dead,
I AM the God who will come again,
I AM Jesus Christ, the Son of God,
I AM the one who died for you and forgives your sins,
I AM ... your God, your God!

I AM the Holy Spirit who leads you by the hand,
I AM the one who brings to you the joy of new life,
I AM the one who knows all things and gives you gifts.
I AM the one who sees your heart and sees your mind
I AM who fills you with wisdom and knowledge sublime!
I AM ...Your God, your God!

Know that I will always be your God,
You can come to me at any time...
Repenting of what is in your heart and on your mind.
I will always love you...always love you... child of mine!
I AM ... Your God, your God!

WORD OF GOD

Acts 10:41, "To us who were chosen by God as witnesses, who ate and drank with him after he rose from the dead."

Psalm 103:2-3, "Bless the LORD, O my soul, and forget not all his benefits, who forgives all your iniquity,"

Jeremiah 20:12, "O LORD of hosts, who tries the righteous, who sees the heart and the mind ... to thee have I committed my cause."

Hosea 2:19, "And I will betroth you to me forever; I will betroth you to me in righteousness and in justice, in steadfast love, and in mercy."

What am I personally speaking to you through the photograph, reflection and Scripture? During your day I invite you to continue in My presence, remembering those truths I have revealed to you personally, responding to Me by writing to Me what touched your heart.

SECTION 2

God's All-Seeing, All-Knowing, All-Good Love

"O mystic marvel! The universal Father is one, and the universal Word; and the Holy Spirit is one and the same everywhere,"
Clement of Alexandria † A.D. 217

"You, Eternal Trinity, are my Creator, and I am the work of Your hands, and I know through the new creation which You have given me in the blood of Your Son, that You are enamored of the beauty of Your workmanship."
Saint Catherine of Siena † 1380

Artwork on Facing Page: "The Holy Trinity," attributed to Francisco Caro, 1627-1667

I Know Your Heart is Breaking

My Child,

I know your heart is breaking…
    So is Mine.
I know your tears are flowing…
    So are Mine.
I know the pain you are feeling…
    I feel it too.
I know the concerns of your heart…
    I have them too.
I know the desires of your heart…
    I have the same desires.

There is not one sorrow or tear or pain or concern or desire that you have felt…
    That I have not experienced with you. I have known it all…from the beginning.
        Felt it all…from the beginning. From the first moment of conception,
            It was all there before Me…in My heart…in My suffering heart.

I see it all…know it all…endure it all…heal it all…transform it all.
Renew it all…redeem it all…welcome it all…love it all.

It all returns to Me.
Know that all will return to Me.
I have heard your every prayer,
Answered your every need.
So too in this, as in all things,
I will bring joy in the morning.
Your time of sorrow will be no more.
I will wipe every tear away,
And my comfort will surround you to the full.
Be at Peace. Be at Rest. Be at Peace.

WORD OF GOD

Psalm 147:3, "He heals the brokenhearted, and binds up their wounds."

2 Titus 2:12, "If we endure, we shall also reign with him;"

Revelation 7:17, "For the Lamb in the midst of the throne will be their shepherd, and he will guide them to springs of living water; and God will wipe away every tear from their eyes."

Psalm 30:5, "His favor is for a lifetime. Weeping may tarry for the night, but joy comes with the morning."

What am I personally speaking to you through the photograph, reflection and Scripture? During your day I invite you to continue in My presence, remembering those truths I have revealed to you personally, responding to Me by writing to Me what touched your heart.

"This, in short, is the difference between us and others who know not God, that in misfortune they complain and murmur, while the adversity does not call us away from the truth of virtue and faith, but strengthens us by its suffering."

Saint Cyprian † A.D. 258

Words of Eternal Life

Beloved, <u>look</u> at the photograph. What draws your interest? <u>Read</u> the reflection and the Scriptures, <u>reflect</u> upon them, linger, <u>rest</u> and be <u>restored</u> in My Truth. <u>Respond</u> with your heart to Me and <u>remain</u> with Me as I remain with you.

Beloved,

Glorious in riches and majesty am I…
    Above all the earth.
        There is no other.
            From right to left, above and below,

There is nowhere else to go… but to Me.
    My words are words of life.
        There is life in no other.
            You have questions…Ask them.
                You have hurts…They will be healed.
                    There is nowhere else to go but to Me alone.

Come and receive the words of eternal life!

    Rest in Me …And you will truly find rest.

        Abide in Me…And you will wish to abide in no other.

            Delight in Me…And you will delight in no other.

Be encouraged by Me and you will need encouragement from no other.

    Be crucified with Me…And you will rise to life eternal.

        Receive freely what I wish to give to you.

            Give freely because of what has been given unto you.

Begin here!

WORD OF GOD

Psalm 139:7-12, "Whither shall I go from thy Spirit? Or whither shall I flee from thy presence? If I ascend to heaven, thou art there! If I make my bed in Sheol, thou art there! If I take the wings of the morning and dwell in the uttermost parts of the sea, even there thy hand shall lead me, and thy right hand shall hold me. If I say, 'Let only darkness cover me, and the light about me be night,' even the darkness is not dark to thee, the night is bright as the day; for darkness is as light with thee."

Psalm 147:3, "He heals the brokenhearted, and binds up their wounds"

John 12:24, "Truly, truly, I say to you, unless a grain of wheat falls into the earth and dies, it remains alone; but if it dies, it bears much fruit. He who loves his life loses it, and he who hates his life in this world will keep it for eternal life."

Matthew 10:8, "Heal the sick, raise the dead, cleanse lepers, cast out demons. You received without paying, give without pay."

What am I personally speaking to you through the photograph, reflection and Scripture? During your day I invite you to continue in My presence, remembering those truths I have revealed to you personally, responding to Me by writing to Me what touched your heart.

"Eternal Trinity... mystery deep as the sea, You could give me no greater gift than the gift of Yourself. For You are a fire ever burning and never consumed, which itself consumes all the selfish love that fills my being..."

Saint Catherine of Siena, Doctor of the Church † 1380

My Love Never Grows Old

My Child,

Trust in Me. Though others fail you, I will never fail you.
  Though others fail you and do not understand,
    I will always understand.
      Though others are not present in your trials, I am always present.
        My love for you never grows old. My love is ageless,
          Forever new, forever fresh, forever waiting,
            Forever alive and vital, forever true.
              My cross is forever before you,
                My wisdom forever drawing you,
                  My spirit forever calling you.
                    Come drink the waters of life without price.

The fruit of your life now…

    At this time, will be different than it was six months ago,

        Or one year ago, or one month ago.

            Do not expect My spirit to continually be doing the same thing in you.

                My spirit is… continually flowing with life,

                    Continually changing… ever new… new Life.

                    Have hope… because of my new life!

WORD OF GOD

Hebrews 13:5, "Keep your life free from love of money, and be content with what you have; for he has said, "I will never fail you nor forsake you.""

Psalm 63:3, "Because thy steadfast love is better than life, my lips will praise thee."

1 Thessalonians 5:24, "He who calls you is faithful, and he will do it."

Revelations 21:5, "And he who sat upon the throne said, "Behold, I make all things new." Also he said, "Write this, for these words are trustworthy and true."

What am I personally speaking to you through the photograph, reflection and Scripture? During your day I invite you to continue in My presence, remembering those truths I have revealed to you personally, responding to Me by writing to Me what touched your heart.

"On one occasion I was reflecting on the Holy Trinity… on the essence of God. I absolutely wanted to know and fathom who God is…
My spirit was caught up into what seemed to be the next world. I saw an inaccessible light, and in this light what appeared like three sources of light… out of this light came words in the form of lightning which encircled heaven and earth. Not understanding anything, I was very sad. Suddenly, from this sea of inaccessible light came our dearly beloved Savior, unutterably beautiful with His shining Wounds… from this light there came a voice which said, Who God is in His Essence, no one will fathom, neither the mind of angels nor of man. Jesus said to me, Get to know God by contemplating His attributes. A moment later, He traced the sign of the cross with His hand and vanished "

Saint Maria Faustina † 1938

When All Seems Lost

Beloved,

When all seems lost, when all <u>is</u> lost,
>   When the night is dark… I AM still here. I AM still here.
>   When it all seems for naught… I AM still here.

Rescue me oh God and have mercy upon me in the midst of my darkness.

Beloved, you are weathered over, beaten down…
 By a storm of unbelief, now, at this time. When the enemy attacks
  With His lies, put forth a shield of My blood, shed for you on My cross.
   The truth is that out of My love for you, I have permitted…
    Not out of My perfect will, but out of My permissive will…
     What I knew would, or could, bring you to Me more fully…
      To lay forth your life before Me as a holocaust offering,
       Causing you to trust more fully in Me alone.

You too have doubts about your natural gifts given by Me.
 In this also trust in Me, that I have given to you exactly what you need.

Beloved, no more allow the devil to cause havoc with your emotions, or in your
 Belief in who I am to you and for you. I love you My Beloved.
  I say it to you once again…I love you! Rejoice in our love!

Have I not given to you this very day, this very night, as a pure gift?
 Is it not out of My love? Then… Trust Me My Beloved…
  Trust Me My Friend…. Trust Me, Oh My Love,
   Trust Me who lives within you, as you live within Me.
    I am with you always, especially when you are in need.
     Quiet yourself and rest in Me, who loves you always!

WORD OF GOD

Isaiah 65:1, "I was ready to be sought by those who did not ask for me; I was ready to be found by those who did not seek me. I said, "Here am I, here am I," to a nation that did not call on my name."

Hebrews 2:13, "And again, "I will put my trust in him." And again, "Here am I, and the children God has given me."

Psalm 90:4, "For a thousand years in thy sight are but as yesterday when it is past, or as a watch in the night."

Psalm 143:8, "Let me hear in the morning of thy steadfast love, for in thee I put my trust. Teach me the way I should go, for to thee I lift up my soul."

What am I personally speaking to you through the photograph, reflection and Scripture? During your day I invite you to continue in My presence, remembering those truths I have revealed to you personally, responding to Me by writing to Me what touched your heart.

The Shepherd

Beloved, <u>look</u> at the photograph. What draws your interest? <u>Read</u> the reflection and the Scriptures, <u>reflect</u> upon them, linger, <u>rest</u> and be <u>restored</u> in My Truth. <u>Respond</u> with your heart to Me and <u>remain</u> with Me as I remain with you.

My Beloved One,

I carry you when you are in trouble.

 I know when you are tired and I carry you across My shoulder.

  I can feel your heart beating next to Mine.

   I will always take the time to find you.

    I lovingly hold you, so that you feel no pain.

I am careful with you. I am strong and protective of you.

 I will always bring you to a place that is safe. I favor you!

  My favor is upon you because of your, "Yes", to Me.

   The blood of My cross, shed for you, cost Me everything...everything!

    Yes! It cost Me everything...But willingly did I shed it for you,

     My favored little one. I pour a challis of My blood over you...

      With delight, with joy and with jubilation!

Partake of Me and of My shed Blood in the Eucharist. Be fed by Me.
Become one with Me, with My Father and with the Holy Spirit,
Devouring and being devoured in Our love…as One with you…
And you, My little one, as one with Us!

WORD OF GOD

Psalms 4:8, "In peace I will both lie down and sleep; for you alone, O Lord, make me dwell in safety."

Ezekiel 34:16, "I myself will be the shepherd of my sheep, and I will make them lie down, says the Lord God. I will seek the lost, and I will bind up the crippled, and I will strengthen the weak."

Hosea 11:4, "I led them with cords of human kindness, with bands of love. I was to them like those who lift infants to their cheeks. I bent down to them and fed them."

John 10:27-30, "My sheep hear my voice. I know them, and they follow me. I give them eternal life, and they will never perish. No one will snatch them out of my hand. What my Father has given me is greater than all else, and no one can snatch it out of the Father's hand. The Father and I are one."

What am I personally speaking to you through the photograph, reflection and Scripture? During your day I invite you to continue in My presence, remembering those truths I have revealed to you personally, responding to Me by writing to Me what touched your heart.

"There is but one unbegotten Being, God, even the Father;
and one only–begotten Son, God, the Word and man;
and one Comforter, the Spirit of truth; and also one preaching, one faith,
and one baptism;"

Saint Ignatius of Antioch † A.D. 107

"The whole earth is a living icon of the face of God."

St. John of Damascus, Father and Doctor of the Church † A.D. 749

I See You There... I Know You

Beloved,

Glorious in riches and majesty am I…
 Above all the earth there is no other.
  From right to left, above and below,

There is nowhere else to go… but to Me. My words are words of life!
 There is life in no other. You have questions…Ask them.
  You have hurts…They will be healed.
   There is nowhere else to go but to Me alone.
    Come and receive the words of eternal life!
     Rest in Me …and you will truly find rest.
      Abide in Me…and you will wish to abide in no other.
       Delight in Me…and you will delight in no other.

Be encouraged by Me and encouragement will be needed from no other.
 Be crucified with Me… And you will rise to life eternal.
  Receive freely what I wish to give to you.
   Give freely because of what has been given unto you.
    Begin here, Beloved!

You will see…You will hear…You will touch…You will know it is Me!
 Because it will be Me…all Three! Something new…something old…
  Something yet to be told… Something ready now to unfold…
   See it comes into your midst…A surprise of love…A surprise of joy!

Always something new to behold. Always will there be…for all eternity.
 As you continually come to know Me. Mystery…because it is Me…all Three!

WORD OF GOD

Psalm 139:7-12, "Whither shall I go from thy Spirit? Or whither shall I flee from thy presence? If I ascend to heaven, thou art there! If I make my bed in Sheol, thou art there! If I take the wings of the morning and dwell in the uttermost parts of the sea, even there thy hand shall lead me, and thy right hand shall hold me. If I say, 'Let only darkness cover me, and the light about me be night,' even the darkness is not dark to thee, the night is bright as the day; for darkness is as light with thee."

Matthew 10:8, "Heal the sick, raise the dead, cleanse lepers, cast out demons. You received without paying, give without pay."

Colossians 1:27, "To them God chose to make known how great among the Gentiles are the riches of the glory of this mystery, which is Christ in you, the hope of glory."

What am I personally speaking to you through the photograph, reflection and Scripture? During your day I invite you to continue in My presence, remembering those truths I have revealed to you personally, responding to Me by writing to Me what touched your heart.

"But [the faithful] worship the Father and the Son and the Holy Spirit, one Godhead; God the Father, God the Son and God the Holy Spirit, one nature in three personalities, intellectual, perfect, self-existent, numerically separate, but not separate in godhead."

Saint Gregory Nazianzen † A.D. 389

Do Not Be Grieved, Nor Despair

Beloved, <u>look</u> at the photograph. What draws your interest? <u>Read</u> the reflection and the Scriptures, <u>reflect</u> upon them, linger, <u>rest</u> and be <u>restored</u> in My Truth. <u>Respond</u> with your heart to Me and <u>remain</u> with Me as I remain with you.

Beloved,

At the beginning, did I not have this arranged? Have I not always foreseen...
    And known all? Do I not see now all that is to come, and hold it all...
        In My providence for you and your family, and for all My little ones...
            Who look to Me as Father and Lord? Do I not have even more...
                To give to you? Would I be so small? I Who Am God Almighty
                    Do not limit My glory and power. Be not grieved nor despair,
                        For in your arms you hold a "child", though not so small,
                          Still, in my eyes, a child who is weeping, weeping within.

Weeping though without knowing and without seeing. Yet, I do see.
I have placed this "little one" in your arms to love.
I would not have allowed this circumstance,
Were it not out of love for you and for this "little one" of mine.

The time is short. Be at peace and love. Be at peace and work.
Be at peace and persevere to live out My plan for your life.
In this, you will find fulfillment and My love for you
That is strong and true and dear. Never has there been a time
In the history of the world that I have not answered a prayer.
Nor is there a time that I have ever
Abandoned <u>anyone</u>. I am with you!

I will rescue you…Count on Me…Watch Me do it…Trust in Me!
Easy for Me who knows all things. Do not give up, move on, charge on!
I go before you…I make a way. Come go with Me today!

Persevere! Seek and you will find. Continue on and
I will show you what you are to do. Much work in yet in store for you.
I ask you now to organize…and continue on to do so,
As I continue on before you and with you, My child, My love,
My servant, "bone of My bones and flesh of My flesh". **(Genesis 2:23)**

Beloved, call upon the Holy Spirit to lift you up above all things.
He is One and the same Spirit that is… and was… and will be with you.
He has been with you from the very beginning!

Temptation to sin is forever trying to push its way in…
Like infection around a healthy part of the body.
The only thing that kicks the temptation out of your mind is…
The presence of My Word brought into your mind and heart.
Focus on Me…I am the Word… Focus on My Words of Truth.
Live by My words of Truth. Proclaim them aloud to the tempter.
In My Name! He will flee from you… persevere!
Ask Me to show to you, a Word of My truth,
To carry in your mind each day…
Then use it… live by it…confident in Me,
Confident in the power of My cross,
In My love for you and…
In My Father's love for you!

Here we go! We will finish together. Have no doubt…
Trust Me…There is an end…and then…we will begin again!

THE LONGING, FIERY LOVE OF THE HOLY TRINITY   63

Something new…but something old…Something glorious to behold…
Given to Me…given to you…Given to Our Blessed Mother…
You will see…fulfilling what has been said and asked of thee…
All for Me…upon the tree. Know that I am pleased with Thee!

WORD OF GOD

Lamentations 3:32-33, "But, though he cause grief, he will have compassion according to the abundance of his steadfast love; for he does not willingly afflict or grieve the sons of men."

Matthew 18:14, "So it is not the will of my Father who is in heaven that one of these little ones should perish."

Galatians 6:9, "So let us not grow weary in doing what is right, for we will reap at harvest time, if we do not give up."

Genesis 2:23, "Bone of my bones and flesh of my flesh…"

Colossians 3:12-14, "As God's chosen ones, holy and beloved, clothe yourselves with compassion, kindness, humility, meekness, and patience. [1] Bear with one another and, if anyone has a complaint against another, forgive each other; just as the Lord has forgiven you, so you also must forgive. Above all, clothe yourselves with love, which binds everything together in perfect harmony."

What am I personally speaking to you through the photograph, reflection and Scripture? During your day I invite you to continue in My presence, remembering those truths I have revealed to you personally, responding to Me by writing to Me what touched your heart.

"Moreover, Christians are born for combat,
whereof the greater the vehemence, the more assured,
God willing, the triumph:
'Have confidence; I have overcome the world'" (John 16:33)

Pope Leo XIII † 1903

God's All-Seeing, All-Knowing, All-Good Love

We Will Soar Together

Beloved, <u>look</u> at the photograph. What draws your interest? <u>Read</u> the reflection and the Scriptures, <u>reflect</u> upon them, linger, <u>rest</u> and be <u>restored</u> in My Truth. <u>Respond</u> with your heart to Me and <u>remain</u> with Me as I remain with you.

My Child,

It will be easy, not hard. Be not afraid. I am with you,
 Even unto the end of the age…thus certainly today!
  Enjoy today with its gifts,
   My gifts.
  Enjoy the breezes of the Holy Spirit,
   Gift to you.
  Enjoy the sounds of the many birds,
   Gift to you, my child who loves birds.
  Enjoy the peace,
   Gift to you who are so in need of peace.

See the birds…birds who skim over the top…Just above the rough water?
That is as I want you to do,
Flying just above the rough areas in your life,
Gliding and soaring with My Spirit, lifted above!

Life is short. Do I not care for you even more than these birds?
There is so much more in heaven,
Of which this is only a part; only a part of My heart.
We will soar together, you and I!
There are no favorites in heaven.
Each one of you is an <u>integral</u> part of My heart!

Stay above the rough sea…Soar above it!
Don't be sucked in. The enemy wishes to drown you…
Soar above it all… and wait upon Me!
Do not be discouraged…take the next step…continue on.
Move forward…Trust Me to bring all to a finish.
Just keep moving…Be not afraid.
Be bold in Me…Be led by Me.
It is to be done all
In Me.

What is there to fear…
When it is done…
All in Me…
By Me…and
For Me?

Who is there to judge you but Me alone?
Let not the enemy deter you from doing what is…
My direction…My leading…My love for you.

I Am Who I Am, is with you!
All in "Oneness…Being…Three in One".
All glory given to One.
All power given to One.
All love given to One.
I Am One…given as three…
Given as Hope for eternity.
One…given as three…
So you will have and
Understand more of Me!

Song of Songs 8:7, "Many waters cannot quench love, neither can floods drown it."

Matthew 14:24, 30-33, "But the boat by this time was many furlongs distant from the land, beaten by the waves; for the wind was against them…but when he saw the wind, he was afraid, and beginning to sink he cried out, "Lord, save me. Jesus immediately reached out his hand and caught him, saying to him, 'O man of little faith, why did you doubt?' And when they got into the boat, the wind ceased. And those in the boat worshiped him, saying, 'Truly you are the Son of God.'"

Matthew 6:26, "Look at the birds of the air: they neither sow nor reap nor gather into barns, and yet your heavenly Father feeds them. Are you not of more value than they?"

John 3:8, "The wind blows where it wills, and you hear the sound of it, but you do not know whence it comes or whither it goes; so it is with everyone who is born of the Spirit."

Exodus 3:14, "God said to Moses, "I AM WHO I AM." He said further, "Thus you shall say to the Israelites, 'I AM has sent me to you.'"

What am I personally speaking to you through the photograph, reflection and Scripture? During your day I invite you to continue in My presence, remembering those truths I have revealed to you personally, responding to Me by writing to Me what touched your heart.

"In the heart of Jesus, which was pierced,
the kingdom of heaven and the land of earth are bound together.
Here is for us the source of life.
This heart is the heart of the Triune Divinity,
and the center of all human hearts…
It draws us to itself with secret power,
it conceals us in itself in the Father's bosom and floods us with the
Holy Spirit.
This heart, it beats for us in a small tabernacle
where it remains mysteriously hidden
in that still, white host."

Saint Teresa Benedicta of the Cross (Edith Stein) † 1942

Though You Do Not Understand, Yet Still I Can Work

My Child,

Though you do not understand,
> Yet still I can work.
>> Though you do not have all the answers,
>>> Yet still I work.
>>>> Though you are lost or alone,
>>>>> Yet still I can work.

Though life did not turn out as you expected, yet still I can work.
> It is in your aloneness and in humility,
>> That I can manifest My glory.
>>> In the aloneness and humility of the cross
>>>> Was My greatest glory given to the Father.

I was so very happy to please Him. Can you be so happy to please Me?
Happy to embrace this time of aloneness, this time of humility?
It is through this time that My will will be done.

I love you My child. Be at peace and rest in Me.
Be not anxious or afraid, for I am with you.
Get on with what needs to be done and be finished with it,
So the important things can be done.
Where is the desire of your heart?

I love you My child. I will be with you and teach you to love Me in others,
For I am there…as I am in you….to love and be loved this day.
Go forth to love, and you will be loving Me within others, as you love each one.
I go with you. I never give you more than I give strength for the day.

WORD OF GOD

Philippians 2:5-8, "Have this mind among yourselves, which is yours in Christ Jesus, who, though he was in the form of God, did not count equality with God a thing to be grasped, but emptied himself, taking the form of a servant, being born in the likeness of men."

Philippians 2:13, "For God is at work in you, both to will and to work for his good pleasure."

Psalm 23:4, "Even though I walk through the valley of the shadow of death, I fear no evil; for thou art with me; thy rod and thy staff, they comfort me."

Isaiah 55:8, 9, 11, "For my thoughts are not your thoughts, neither are your ways my ways, says the LORD. For as the heavens are higher than the earth, so are my ways higher than your ways and my thoughts than your thoughts….so shall my word be that goes forth from my mouth; it shall not return to me empty, but it shall accomplish that which I purpose, and prosper in the thing for which I sent it."

What am I personally speaking to you through the photograph, reflection and Scripture?
During your day I invite you to continue in My presence, remembering those truths I have
revealed to you personally, responding to Me by writing to Me what touched your heart.

You Are Never Alone

Beloved,

I am there at each turn.
>You are never alone…
>>Never abandoned.
>>>Could you abandon your own child?
>>>>Of course not. Nor could I.

I have given you all that you need to succeed and to have abundance:
I give to you Hope, because without Me... you have no Hope.
I give to you Love, because without Me...you have no Love.
I give to you Faith, because without Me... you have no Faith.
I give to you all things, out of My love for you...My Dear One.

I go before you...Be bold! I walk with you. Be not afraid
All is for good...All is needed...All is for good...Be still in Me.
Time and space have no meaning here, only love.
Have you loved?...Is there love toward others?...Love toward Me?
Love is to be brimming over, full of giving...
A giving of heart and mind and out of ones needs...
Not all of ones needs, but out of ones needs.
I have called you to be holy.
What is it to be holy?

Is it not to do what the Father asks of you? Let there be this day a triumph of
My cross in your life...so that from this day forth you shall experience
More of My resurrection! There will be now an aroma of My holiness...
Ever more, until I come in glory! Always there are new beginnings
For all mankind. The sun rises new every morning and always
There is rest...Rest in Me...Let Me...Follow Me...
Listen to Me...Trust in Me My Beloved.

WORD OF GOD

---

1 Peter 1:3, "His divine power has granted to us all things that pertain to life and godliness, through the knowledge of him who called us to his own glory and excellence."

Romans 8:38-39, "For I am sure that neither death, nor life, nor angels, nor principalities, nor things present, nor things to come, nor powers, nor height, nor depth, nor anything else in all creation, will be able to separate us from the love of God in Christ Jesus our LORD."

What am I personally speaking to you through the photograph, reflection and Scripture? During your day I invite you to continue in My presence, remembering those truths I have revealed to you personally, responding to Me by writing to Me what touched your heart.

I Will Never Leave You Orphaned

My Child,

I will never leave you alone. I am with you always…

Even until the end of the age… I will never leave you orphaned.

Does a mother forget her baby, a woman the child from within her womb?

Know that I am with you as you persevere. In My presence there is life!

Grace begets grace, which begets more grace, as you draw closer to Me.
I desire for you to be with Me where I am…and where I am is glory.

The more you draw close to Me…the more you will reside in My glory.
My desire is for you to have more of Me…and for Me to have more of you!
I draw you closer to My Father …with Me.
Trust Me…Trust Me…Trust Me…Trust Me…Trust Me…Trust Me.
In all things trust Me! Will you trust Me? Can you trust Me?
Just trust Me…as I have loved you and trusted you, My Child.
Always am I faithful!

Dear Lord,
Various times in life flash through my mind.
I think I am alone but You are there looking at me through Your eyes.
I am not alone…
You are there watching, guarding, waiting, giving me time.
In the same way our children can think they are alone,
Yet our love, concern, attention, prayers, support,
affection surrounds them…
So do Yours surround me… and them.

WORD OF GOD

John 14:18, "I will not leave you desolate; I will come to you."

Psalm 139:1-6, "O LORD, thou hast searched me and known me! Thou knowest when I sit down and when I rise up; thou discernest my thoughts from afar. Thou searchest out my path and my lying down, and art acquainted with all my ways. Even before a word is on my tongue, lo, O LORD, thou knowest it altogether. Thou dost beset me behind and before, and layest thy hand upon me. Such knowledge is too wonderful for me"

Isaiah 49:15, "Can a woman forget her sucking child, that she should have no compassion on the son of her womb? Even these may forget, yet I will not forget you."

What am I personally speaking to you through the photograph, reflection and Scripture? During your day I invite you to continue in My presence, remembering those truths I have revealed to you personally, responding to Me by writing to Me what touched your heart.

The First Shall Be Last

My Child,

You have lovingly prepared your gift of service for Me.
    Is this not how I give things unto you?...
        Each gift lovingly prepared and given freely.
            Now I am taking your carefully prepared gift of service
            And giving it to others to finish the task.
                Is this not what you asked My child,

    God's All-Seeing, All-Knowing, All-Good Love

That you be made My servant?
Have I not answered your prayers?

Does a servant choose how he serves his master?...
Or rather serve him in love and obedience...
In whatever manner the master chooses.
Is it service to the master, or rather self service
When the servant chooses what he would do?
How can you best know how I would use you,
When you know not all things?

Have I not said, "The first shall be last and the last shall be first."?
Who are you to choose when you shall be first and when you shall be last?
There has been a time when I have put you first,
And now comes a time when I have placed you last.
Shall not the first be last?

But there shall come a time when I shall place you first again.
Shall not the last be first?
Judge not My motives but rather My love.
Can you not recall that, "God is love."?
Choose not how or when you will serve,
But rather say "Yes" to service.

Hold not to the things of this world but rather to Me.
I give material things as gifts,
But you are not to hold fast to them.
Rather count them as blessings that belong to Me.

Mine to give; mine to take.
Yours to receive; yours to give,
A gift of pure love that you have lovingly prepared.
Is this not how I give things unto you?

Does a servant choose when he is to have leisure
And when he is to have work?
Know not I all things?
Do I work not all things for your good?
Trust Me My child.
Trust Me.
I love you!

This will be a time of peace for you,
For you shall know the peace that comes from doing My will.
You shall know the freedom and joy I have promised to you!

WORD OF GOD

1 Corinthians 3:10, "According to the grace of God given to me, like a skilled master builder I laid a foundation, and another man is building upon it. Let each man take care how he builds upon it."

Mark 10:31, "But many that are first will be last, and the last first."

Job 1:21, "And he said, 'Naked I came from my mother's womb, and naked shall I return; the LORD gave, and the LORD has taken away; blessed be the name of the LORD.'"

Jeremiah 17:7, "Blessed is the man who trusts in the LORD, whose trust is the LORD."

What am I personally speaking to you through the photograph, reflection and Scripture? During your day I invite you to continue in My presence, remembering those truths I have revealed to you personally, responding to Me by writing to Me what touched your heart.

"Therefore,
neither would the Lord, nor the Holy Spirit, nor the apostles,
have ever named as God,
definitely and absolutely, him who was not God,
unless he were truly God;
nor would they have named any one in his own person Lord,
except God the Father ruling over all,
and His Son who has received dominion from His Father over
all creation, as this passage has it:
"The Lord said unto my Lord,
Sit Thou at my right hand, until I make Thine enemies Thy footstool."
Here the [Scripture] represents to us the Father addressing the Son;
He who gave Him the inheritance of the heathen,
and subjected to Him all His enemies.
Since, therefore, the Father is truly Lord, and the Son truly Lord,
the Holy Spirit has fitly designated them by the title of Lord."

Saint Ireneaus † A.D. 202

Use This Time for My Word

Beloved, <u>look</u> at the photograph. What draws your interest? <u>Read</u> the reflection and the Scriptures, <u>reflect</u> upon them, linger, <u>rest</u> and be <u>restored</u> in My Truth. <u>Respond</u> with your heart to Me and <u>remain</u> with Me as I remain with you.

Beloved,

Know Me by uniting with Me each day!
Become one through the day with My Word and with My Spirit.
Use this time for My word…this time that is quiet and still.
Be still and know that I am the Word and I am within you today!

Walk with Me…
Talk with Me…
Follow Me…
Be not anxious or afraid.
I fill your life…
With the communion of saints and
Angels in your midst!

Prepared are you…Beyond prepared…
Loved are you…Beyond loved…
Graced are you…Beyond graced.
Speak that which I speak to you.
No more… No less.
It will be enough!
I go before you…
To show to you the Way…
My way!

Know it is My work…I will accomplish all that still needs to be accomplished.
It is My work. I will show to you the way today…even today. Be at peace.
Prepare…Move forward…I am waiting at the end to give to you
A heavenly reward…grace…upon grace… upon grace.
I love you. I am with you. Trust Me!

I go before you My Little One…
It is I, the Lord.
Fear not! Be amazed…
At the work of My hand.

There will be a finish…
Do I not finish all things well? In My time…it will come.
In My will it will be done. Wait upon Me…Trust Me.
Be not anxious or afraid. I am the Lord!

WORD OF GOD

John 8:31, "Jesus then said…If you continue in my word, you are truly my disciples,"

Psalm 139:3, "Thou searchest out my path and my lying down, and art acquainted with all my ways."

God's All-Seeing, All-Knowing, All-Good Love

Deuteronomy 33:1-3, "This is the blessing with which Moses the man of God blessed the children of Israel before his death. He said, 'The LORD… he came from the ten thousands of holy ones, with flaming fire at his right hand. Yea, he loved his people; all those consecrated to him were in his hand; so they followed in thy steps, receiving direction from thee,'"

Hebrews 12:1, "Therefore, since we are surrounded by so great a cloud of witnesses, let us also lay aside every weight, and sin which clings so closely, and let us run with perseverance the race that is set before us,"

Psalm 91:11, "For he will give his angels charge of you to guard you in all your ways."

Jeremiah 23:24, "Can a man hide himself in secret places so that I cannot see him? says the LORD. Do I not fill heaven and earth? says the LORD."

Psalm 118:1, "O give thanks to the LORD, for he is good; his steadfast love endures for ever!"

What am I personally speaking to you through the photograph, reflection and Scripture? During your day I invite you to continue in My presence, remembering those truths I have revealed to you personally, responding to Me by writing to Me what touched your heart.

"I understand the spiritual espousal of a soul with God, which has no exterior manifestation. It is a purely interior act between the soul and God. This grace has drawn me into the very burning center of God's love. I have come to understand His Trinitarian quality and the absolute Oneness of His Being."

"His Trinitarian Being enveloped me entirely."

Saint Maria Faustina † 1938

"In Christ Jesus our Lord, by whom and with whom be glory and power to the Father with the Holy Spirit forever."

**Saint Ignatius of Antioch, Apostolic Father of the
Early Church, and Bishop of Antioch † A.D. 108**

Your Heart is Mine

Beloved, <u>look</u> at the photograph. What draws your interest? <u>Read</u> the reflection and the Scriptures, <u>reflect</u> upon them, linger, <u>rest</u> and be <u>restored</u> in My Truth. <u>Respond</u> with your heart to Me and <u>remain</u> with Me as I remain with you.

My Child,

Your heart is Mine…Your soul is Mine…
Your spirit, Mine as well.
I hold you close…I see your heart…
I see your mind, full well.
I was there with you as you lay in the sun,
I was there with you in the shade of the tree,
When you again reached out to me

You are Mine, My child…I have loved you well.
Your heart is being transformed…transformed to look and think like Me.
Come, love Me now…Sit at My knee.

God's All-Seeing, All-Knowing, All-Good Love

Come, know Me now…Draw close to Me.
My name is Jesus,
My name is Lord,
My name is Father,
Holy One, I Am Who Am, One to be adored.

Come sing with Me…Come dance with Me…
Let joy fill your heart and soul. Let My Spirit guide you…
Lead you… teach you. Come, eternity awaits you.
Come, it is I who await you, I Am…I Am your Lord!

You are not alone…Be not afraid! Ask Me now…Just ask Me…
And I will come in and dwell with you,
Lay your sorrowing head upon My chest,
And then come…dwell <u>within</u> Me…as your Lord!

WORD OF GOD

1 Samuel 16:7, "For the LORD sees not as man sees; man looks on the outward appearance but the LORD looks on the heart."

Ephesians 3:16-20, "That according to the riches of his glory he may grant you to be strengthened with might through his Spirit in the inner man, and that Christ may dwell in your hearts through faith; that you, being rooted and grounded in love, may have power to comprehend with all the saints what is the breadth and length and height and depth, and to know the love of Christ which surpasses knowledge, that you may be filled with all the fullness of God. Now to him who by the power at work within us is able to do far more abundantly than all that we ask or think,"

Psalm 23:6, "Surely goodness and mercy shall follow me all the days of my life; and I shall dwell in the house of the LORD for ever."

What am I personally speaking to you through the photograph, reflection and Scripture? During your day I invite you to continue in My presence, remembering those truths I have revealed to you personally, responding to Me by writing to Me what touched your heart.

"Listen and attend with the ear of your heart."

Saint Benedict † A.D. 547

God's Infinite Design as Creator

"There is one God of the universe, the Father of Christ, "of whom are all things;" and also one Holy Spirit, who wrought in Moses, and in the prophets and apostles:"
Saint Ignatius of Antioch † A.D. 107

"Talk to the Three Persons, to God the Father, to God the Son, to God the Holy Spirit. And so as to reach the Blessed Trinity, go through Mary."
Saint Josemaría Escrivá † 1975

"Although he was God, he took flesh; and having been made man, he remained what he was: God." **Saint Origen † A.D. 254**

Artwork on Facing Page: "The Holy Trinity," Pieter Coecke Van Aeist, 1527 -1559

My Family

My Child,

It is <u>My Family</u> that is the JOY of My Life.
It is <u>My Family</u> that is the focus…
The center of all the heavens! <u>My Family</u>!
WE ARE FAMILY!
Father, Son and Holy Spirit!
Family with My Mother Mary,
Family with My Guardian Joseph…
My Heavenly Family…
My earthly Family…
<u>All one family</u>.

<u>Family</u> is the key to all eternity! <u>Family</u> is your <u>only</u> hope to be one with Me…
Seek out <u>My</u> Family! We are as a Tree…A Tree of Life…
A Tree of Hope…All together…Waiting for you…<u>My Family</u>!

God's Infinite Design as Creator

Where is My Family on this earth?
Is it in your heart, my home in you?
Is it in your church?
Is it in your loved ones? Those I have gifted to you?
My child, it is in all three!
Will you now be one with Me…
One with My Family on this earth and
One with My Heavenly Family?
My heavenly Family is… The Tree of Eternity,
The Father, The Son, and The Holy Spirit!

We are all one within you, and We are one within
My Blessed earthly Holy Family…
My Mother Mary, My Guardian Joseph and My Church.
Come! Come and you will see!
Come and you will see there…
In the loving mix of family
What I have longed to share with you
From the beginning of eternity!

There at that moment you stood before The Tree,
The Tree of the Knowledge of Good and Evil and
The Tree of Life that is Me…and decided to disobey Me…
I had already prepared for you…
My earthly family and your earthly family,
And it is My Heavenly Family <u>and</u> My earthly Family
Together…that will now bring you home to Me!

I am <u>HOLY</u>!
<u>I Am and Was and Will always be</u>…
The burning bush…The burning tree…My Heart burning…
With love for you…Yes All Three…The Trinity.
I was testing you. <u>Do you now see</u>? I was testing,
As a Father does… a much loved son or daughter.
So I could see, as I had hoped, that you would obey Me…
So we could <u>truly</u> be a Family!
I have never left you alone…
I was <u>always</u> there and am now…
Always there with you. Do you now see?
<u>I had prepared from the start,</u>
As a Father does, that we would never be apart,
That you would never be far from My Heart…
My Burning Heart…that burns with love for you!

And now it is the love within My Holy Family...
    That will FINALLY bring you home to Me!
        I have waited long and I now rejoice...
            In your love for Me, and for My Family!

WORD OF GOD

Ephesians 3:14-17, "For this reason I bow my knees before the Father, from whom every family in heaven and on earth is named, that according to the riches of his glory he may grant you to be strengthened with might through his Spirit in the inner man, and that Christ may dwell in your hearts through faith; that you, being rooted and grounded in love..."

1 Timothy 3:15, "If I am delayed, you may know how one ought to behave in the household of God, which is the church of the living God, the pillar and bulwark of the truth."

Ephesians 5:27-32, "That he might present the church to himself in splendor, without spot or wrinkle or any such thing, that she might be holy and without blemish. For no man ever hates his own flesh, but nourishes and cherishes it, as Christ does the church. This mystery is a profound one, and I am saying that it refers to Christ and the church..."

What am I personally speaking to you through the photograph, reflection and Scripture? During your day I invite you to continue in My presence, remembering those truths I have revealed to you personally, responding to Me by writing to Me what touched your heart.

"We do not confess three Gods but one God in three persons, the 'consubstantial Trinity.'
The divine persons do not share the one divinity among themselves but each of them is God whole and entire.
In the words of the Fourth Lateran Council (1215),
"Each of the persons is that supreme reality, the divine substance, essence or nature."

The Trinity within the Family

Beloved, <u>look</u> at the photograph. What draws your interest? <u>Read</u> the reflection and the Scriptures, <u>reflect</u> upon them, linger, <u>rest</u> and be <u>restored</u> in My Truth. <u>Respond</u> with your heart to Me and <u>remain</u> with Me as I remain with you.

Lord, how can I relate to You now?
Lord, where are You in my life?
Lord, teach me about how a husband and wife are
"together under God."

My Child,

The trinity of the family, the husband and wife under God,
 Rests together as one within the Most Holy Trinity.
  The husband is to be submissive to God, and the wife is the husband's
   Helpmate in accomplishing the leading of God's will for them as a family.
    In a baptized, spiritual relationship with God,
     Womankind is set free from bondage and is with man...
      Together... under God.

"Craving for him", is sanctified into desire to please him and to be unified with him.
 "Subject to him" is sanctified to "submission to him,"
  Yet with dignity; being unified...
   Together as Jesus Christ to God the Father is submissive,
    Yet unified with Him by the love of the Holy Spirit.
     The love of the Holy Spirit flows through the Father's love
      And His care for the Son, and then, in return,
       The Holy Spirit flows through the Son's love
        And respect for the Father.

In the same way, the Holy Spirit flows through a husband's love
 As he cares for His wife and in return, the Holy Spirit flows
  Through a wife's love, as she respects her husband.

WORD OF GOD

---

1 Colossians 15:27-28, "'For God has put all things in subjection under his feet.' But when it says, 'All things are put in subjection under him,' it is plain that he is excepted who put all things under him. When all things are subjected to him, then the Son himself will also be subjected to him who put all things under him, that God may be everything to everyone."

Ephesians 5:28, 32-33, "Even so husbands should love their wives as their own bodies. He who loves his wife loves himself...This mystery is a profound one, and I am saying that it refers to Christ and the church; however, let each one of you love his wife as himself, and let the wife see that she respects her husband."

Peter 5:6, "Humble yourselves therefore under the mighty hand of God, that in due time he may exalt you."

What am I personally speaking to you through the photograph, reflection and Scripture? During your day I invite you to continue in My presence, remembering those truths I have revealed to you personally, responding to Me by writing to Me what touched your heart.

God's Infinite Design as Creator

A CHARGE TO YOUNG HUSBANDS IN THE CATHOLIC CATECHISM

"Say this to your young wife:
'I have taken you in my arms, and I love you,
and I prefer you to my life itself.
For the present life is nothing,
and my most ardent dream is to spend it with you
in such a way that we may be assured
of not being separated in the life reserved for us...
I place your love above all things,
and nothing would be more bitter or painful to me
than to be of a different mind than you.'"

Saint John Chrysostom, Bishop and Doctor of the Church † A.D. 322

"I have found you,
and I intend to give myself totally
in order to form a truly Christian family."

"Our body is a cenacle, a monstrance:
Through its crystal the world should see God."

"The secret of happiness is to live moment by moment
and to thank God for all that He is in His goodness
sends to us day after day."

Saint Gianna Beratta Molla, Pediatric Physician, Wife, Mother and Saint
Feast Day ~ April 28, 1962

I Wish to Speak to You About Myself Within the Trinity

Beloved, <u>look</u> at the photograph. What draws your interest? <u>Read</u> the reflection and the Scriptures, <u>reflect</u> upon them, linger, <u>rest</u> and be <u>restored</u> in My Truth. <u>Respond</u> with your heart to Me and <u>remain</u> with Me as I remain with you.

"The Coronation of Mother Mary by the Holy Trinity" at the Sanctuary of Fatima in Portugal

Beloved,

I AM the Word of God made flesh.

    I AM the Word of God that goes forth and creates.

        I AM the Truth.

God's Infinite Design as Creator

I AM a separate identity from the Father or the Holy Spirit.
I AM Christ the second person of the Trinity,
Who chose to become a man, flesh, and to give up My rights as God.
I AM equal with the Father.
The Holy Spirit is equal with the Father and with Me.
We are one because we always seek…
To do the Father's will.

You become one with Me, My child,
As you seek to do the Father's will.
You become one with your brothers and sisters in Christ…
As you seek to do My will,
And they seek to do My will.

My kingdom is coming! Allow Me to reign now in your mind and heart.
Always I ask, "Where is the heart of My Bride today?"
I must wait to return until the heart of My Bride is prepared and ready.
Beloved, what are you doing today to prepare My Bride?
I need workers to plant, workers to till the soil…
And workers to harvest…one with Me.

Be serious in your labor to love and serve Me…
As you love and serve those whom I call you to care for…
That you will bear much fruit, My Beloved.
I long for you…I long for My children to be saved…
I long for My church to be made whole…
I long for My Bride to be one with Me.

Has this not always been the way…
To live in "a good conscience"?
But the flesh wants its own ways…its own conscience.
See the peace, order and joy that comes with My ways?
I AM … all in all…There is no other!
Joy is in Me alone. Rejoice!

Beloved, I long for you to know joy and freedom in Me!
Be set free in Me as you live life being led by the Holy Spirit.
Come let us run together!
Come run within My leading and My love…
My fiery love that longs for you!

Dear Lord Jesus Christ,
I claim so quickly and easily what you, Jesus, did not claim…
my own will and living in my own desires…
rather that the Father's will and desires for me.
Forgive me Dear Lord.
Have mercy upon my weakness…
my idolatry of myself.

WORD OF GOD

John 1:1-4, "In the beginning was the Word, and the Word was with God, and the Word was God. He was in the beginning with God; all things were made through him, and without him was not anything made that was made. In him was life, and the life was the light of men."

John 14:6, "Jesus said to him, " I AM the way, and the truth, and the life; no one comes to the Father, but by me."

1 Timothy 1:18-19, "I am giving you these instructions,… so that by following them you may fight the good fight, having faith and a good conscience. By rejecting conscience, certain persons have suffered shipwreck in the faith;"

Philippians 2:5-8, "Have this mind among yourselves, which is yours in Christ Jesus, who, though he was in the form of God, did not count equality with God a thing to be grasped, but emptied himself, taking the form of a servant, being born in the likeness of men. And being found in human form he humbled himself and became obedient unto death, even death on a cross."

What am I personally speaking to you through the photograph, reflection and Scripture? During your day I invite you to continue in My presence, remembering those truths I have revealed to you personally, responding to Me by writing to Me what touched your heart.

"Faith does not quench desire, but inflames it."

Saint Thomas Aquinas † 1274

God's Infinite Design as Creator

Trust Me

Beloved, <u>look</u> at the photograph. What draws your interest? <u>Read</u> the reflection and the Scriptures, <u>reflect</u> upon them, linger, <u>rest</u> and be <u>restored</u> in My Truth. <u>Respond</u> with your heart to Me and <u>remain</u> with Me as I remain with you.

"Joan of Arc" Dante Gabriel Rosetti, 1882

My "Little One",

Now that you know more of who I am! Can you understand more now
Why I wish all men to really know Me…not to just know of Me?
I am not a God of one dimension…The Love of God the Father…

Rather I Am Three Dimensions, Three Persons in One God Almighty.
And I have ALL the facets of Life within Me!

Would I lead you astray? Would I teach you what you do not need to know?
No! My love is purposed, effectual, mighty as a two edged sword,
Discerning, dividing between Spirit and flesh, between bone and marrow.
To accomplish My will… on My day…in My time.

You have learned more about "littleness", to trust that My timing is best.
You have learned that in Me there is boldness within you that can lead others
To respond to Me…not you yourself, but Me within you.
This is what Joan of Arc spoke with, boldness that was from Me.
Was the result perceived as perfect? No, quite the opposite!
But for the day and for the time she did what I asked of her.
Hers was a Saintly response. Joan's proclamation to troops
Rallied their hearts, minds and wills. For Joan
There was persecution, grief, imprisonment, trial,
A proclamation of what I had revealed…
That she might lead in wisdom and Truth,
The hearts and minds of men who
Were about to go into battle.

Then again in a Court of Law Joan boldly spoke the Truth.
She was built up in boldness through the Saints who spoke to her.
Boldness was needed, not only Truth but Truth proclaimed in boldness.
What was the result? Joan was burned at the stake for heresy!
Without boldness, My Truth placed within Joan,
Would just have been My Truth residing in her heart,
Placed within her by Me. Boldness was what was needed
In order for My Truth to pierce the darkness.
Boldness without faith is only boldness…
But boldness with Faith is what is needed.
From what does boldness come?

It springs forth from the infused virtue of Fortitude.
Fortitude is what is lacking in My people. Be courageous to proclaim boldly
My truth. This is the courage that was spoken of in the bible.
Their courage to boldly proclaim the gospel and live the gospel
Brought them to martyrdom and glorifying My Father.
They had to partake of the boldness that flows forth from
The Holy Spirit. Be bold when I ask you for boldness!
Staying "little" within, let My boldness come forth!
Out of "littleness" My Mother's, "Yes!" was bold

God's Infinite Design as Creator

In Her desire to be "the servant of the Lord".
So too do I call you My "Little One",
To a holy boldness!

WORD OF GOD

John 1:4, "In Him was life, And the life Was the light of Men."

1 Peter 5:6, "Humble yourselves therefore under the mighty hand of God, that in due time he may exalt you."

1 Samuel 3:10,19, "Now the LORD came and stood there, calling as before, "Samuel! Samuel!" And Samuel said, "Speak, for your servant is listening... As Samuel grew up, the LORD was with him and let none of his words fall to the ground."

Acts 4:29, "And now, Lord, look at their threats, and grant to your servants to speak your word with all boldness,"

Acts 4:31, "When they had prayed, the place in which they were gathered together was shaken; and they were all filled with the Holy Spirit and spoke the word of God with boldness."

Acts 4:13, "Now when they saw the boldness of Peter and John and realized that they were uneducated and ordinary men, they were amazed and recognized them as companions of Jesus."

Luke 1:38, "Then Mary said, "Here am I, the servant of the Lord; let it be with me according to your word.""

What am I personally speaking to you through the photograph, reflection and Scripture? During your day I invite you to continue in My presence, remembering those truths I have revealed to you personally, responding to Me by writing to Me what touched your heart.

"I know well that the greater and more beautiful the work is, the more terrible will be the storms that rage against it."

Saint Maria Faustina † 1938

Frustration is Not of Me

My Child,

Frustration is not of Me but of the evil one,
  For so too did he (the devil) become frustrated with his own plans and desires
    That were not My plans and desires,
      And so too did he not yield to My will for him.
        Further could I see than he could see.
        Further can I see than you can see.

Rest in Me… Labor not…Love much.
　　Rejoice in your salvation…Pray for the world.
　　　　Listen to Me in silence…
　　　　　　Listen for the cord of silence… within the quiet.
　　　　　　　　It is My call… a silent yes to My Father…
　　　　　　　　　　To giving all… out of love.

Run not here and there,
　　But wait for the day of My coming,
　　　　Which will come in the blinking of an eye.

Grow in expectation of My coming.
　　Prepare for it, as you would prepare for a fine dinner,
　　　　With all the ingredients planned ahead to bring honor to your guest…
　　　　　　So too will this bring to Me honor and glory at My final coming.

WORD OF GOD

Isaiah 30:18, "Therefore the Lord waits to be gracious to you; therefore, he exalts himself to show mercy to you. For the Lord is a God of justice; blessed are all those who wait for him."

2 Timothy 4:8, "Henceforth there is laid up for me the crown of righteousness, which the Lord, the righteous judge, will award to me on that Day, and not only to me but also to all who have loved his appearing."

Matthew 24: 42, 44, "Watch therefore, for you do not know on what day your Lord is coming… for the Son of man is coming at an hour you do not expect."

What am I personally speaking to you through the photograph, reflection and Scripture?
During your day I invite you to continue in My presence, remembering those truths I have
revealed to you personally, responding to Me by writing to Me what touched your heart.

"Teach us to give and not count the cost."
Saint Ignatius of Loyola † 1556

I Am For You, Not Against You

Beloved, <u>look</u> at the photograph. What draws your interest? <u>Read</u> the reflection and the Scriptures, <u>reflect</u> upon them, linger, <u>rest</u> and be <u>restored</u> in My Truth. <u>Respond</u> with your heart to Me and <u>remain</u> with Me as I remain with you.

My Child,

Since the beginning of time have I planned to call you home to visit Me this day,
    Home with Me… to begin again… I am here for you.
        I <u>have</u> been here for you.
            I will continue to be here for you… because
                I am <u>for</u> you, not against you,
                    <u>For</u> you, to bring you into the fullness of Life.

I would speak to you as a little child.
  Come to Me that I may form you as a Father forms a child,
    As a Father forms his precious, much loved child!
      Come after Me! …Chase after Me!
        One step at a time. Go forth and prepare to find Me!
          One step at a time…It is simple…Keep it simple.
          One step at a time…Walk in My mercy.
              Go to confession to a holy priest...My gift to you!

Eternity knows no bounds nor limits, nor do I,
  Nor do you know bounds or limits in My love,
    That is poured upon you in the blood of My Son Jesus Christ.
      There is nothing I have held back from you, not even one good,
        So total is My love for you, so complete is My care for you,
        So boundless is My vision for you.
            "Eye has not seen, nor ear heard of the love that I have
              For you… And this love comes to you through
                My Son, Christ Jesus your Lord and Savior.
                There is no other…none but Him…
                No other Name through which
                    You are called…but His name alone.
                  Kneel before Him.
                    Bow down before Him.
                      Acknowledge His Name
                      And His Lordship
                      Over you!

He is the bridge…He is the Way…He is the truth…He is the life!
  Are you willing to be formed into Him, that you would become
    The image of My Son…in a world that has few that are an image of Him…
      To a world that cannot conceive of His goodness…
        And cannot conceive of His love?
          Are you willing to be formed into His image?
            There will be no room for foolish concerns.
              There will be no room for self centeredness and strife.

Dedication and zeal must fill My house…total abandonment…
  Then being filled with My love and then
    Total abandonment in the giving of My love.
      If you decide to spend love on yourself,
        Then you will squander it…and it will give you no return…
          But only require the more of you…like a bottomless pit…
            That leads to confusion, darkness and desolation.

But if you spend the love that I fill you with…
On the saving of lost souls…
I will fill you up to overflowing…
With treasures of gold.

Repent and turn from your evil ways.
Sin no more…Desire nothing else but Myself alone…
Put away your worldly desires to always have more …
And desire instead to be made into more…to be made into My Bride.
You will have to die within but with your death within …
Comes Resurrection and new life!
I place before you My Son Jesus Christ, who is risen.
I place before you a bridge that reaches across the abyss.
Will you become that bridge or will you instead…
Fall into the abyss?

WORD OF GOD

Romans 8:31, "What then shall we say to this? If God is for us, who is against us?"

Luke 18:1, "Truly, I say to you, whoever does not receive the kingdom of God like a child shall not enter it."

Sirach 4:26, "Do not be ashamed to confess your sins, and do not try to stop the current of a river.

James 5:16, "Therefore, confess your sins to one another, and pray for one another, so that you may be healed. The prayer of the righteous is powerful and effective."

Revelation 3:16, "So, because you are lukewarm, and neither cold nor hot, I am about to spit you out of my mouth."

Amos 6:1-7, "Alas for those who are at ease…and for those who feel secure… Alas for those who lie on beds of ivory, and lounge on their couches…who sing idle songs… who drink wine… and anoint themselves with the finest oils, but are not grieved over the ruin…Therefore they shall now be the first to go into exile, and the revelry of the loungers shall pass away."

Philippians 3:18-21, "For many live as enemies of the cross of Christ; I have often told you of them, and now I tell you even with tears. Their end is destruction; their god is the belly; and their glory is in their shame; their minds are set on earthly things. But our citizenship is in heaven, and it is from there that we are expecting a

God's Infinite Design as Creator

Savior, the Lord Jesus Christ. He will transform the body of our humiliation that it may be conformed to the body of his glory, by the power that also enables him to make all things subject to himself.

Jeremiah 29:11, "For I know the plans I have for you, says the LORD, plans for welfare and not for evil, to give you a future and a hope."

What am I personally speaking to you through the photograph, reflection and Scripture? During your day I invite you to continue in My presence, remembering those truths I have revealed to you personally, responding to Me by writing to Me what touched your heart.

"But the Holy Spirit
does not speak His own things,
but those of Christ, and that not from Himself,
but from the Lord; even as the Lord also announced to us
the things that He received from the Father.
For, says He, "the word which ye hear is not Mine, but the Father's,
who sent Me." And says He of the Holy Spirit,
"He shall not speak of Himself, but whatsoever things
He shall hear from Me."
And He says of Himself to the Father,
"I have," says He, "glorified Thee upon the earth;
I have finished the work which, Thou gavest Me;
I have manifested Thy name to men."
And of the Holy Ghost,
"He shall glorify Me, for He receives of Mine."

Saint Ignatius of Antioch † A.D. 30 - 107
to the Ephesians Chapter IX

"To fall in love with God is the greatest of all romances;
to seek Him, the greatest adventure;
to find Him, the greatest human achievement."
Saint Augustine of Hippo † A.D. 430

Joy is Coming

My Child,

Do you see that I seek to free you?
> Yes, free you...that you yourself can get out of the way...
>> That I may speak easily through you.

What joy the hours that we will spend together, you and I. What joy yet to come.
> I eagerly wait, as I wait upon you to begin. I lead the way...be sure!
>> I know you think it is slow in coming, but...
>>> I come with a plan...My plan. Rejoice!
>>>> You, my child, My love, who had nothing to give <u>but</u> love,
>>>>> Will have much to give, because I AM ALL.

You will see… you will believe.
You will know that it is Me!

My Father,
Humblest of all are Thou oh Father, listening to such as me.
Having granted all to everyone, having granted all to me.
In return receiving so little, My Father, from Me.
Having given all, in giving Your Son to me upon a tree, I ask You once
again for your forgiveness My Father, for me.
Counting Jesus Your Son's sacrifice as worthy to please Thee,
as worthy to wash me, as worthy to comfort Thee in Your love for me,
I had left Thee alone while You were looking high and low for me…out of
Your love and Your concern for me.
Dearest Father, even now, You do still love me.
Even now my Father, You bring me close to Thee to comfort Me.
Humblest of all are Thee, my wonderful, magnificent, loving Father.
Teach me, oh Father, to love Thee,
The way that You love me.

WORD OF GOD

Psalm 27:6, "and I will offer…sacrifices with shouts of joy; I will sing and make melody to the LORD."

Hebrews 2:3, "For still the vision awaits its time; it hastens to the end--it will not lie. If it seem slow, wait for it; it will surely come, it will not delay."

1 Peter 1:6, "In this you rejoice, though now for a little while you may have to suffer various trials,"

Matthew 22:37, "He said to him, 'You shall love the Lord your God with all your heart, and with all your soul, and with all your mind.'"

What am I personally speaking to you through the photograph, reflection and Scripture? During your day I invite you to continue in My presence, remembering those truths I have revealed to you personally, responding to Me by writing to Me what touched your heart.

Detatchment

Beloved,

In detachment you will experience loneliness, if you are not <u>attached</u> to Me…
As I was attached to My Father through My life, through My Passion on the cross,
I was attached to My Father, as you must be attached to Me…
So that loneliness of spirit will not consume your soul.

I give to you My flesh and my blood to consume.
It is real food, real drink for your soul, that you might not die…
That you might not die of loneliness…detached.
Feed on Me that you might have LIFE to the full…
JOY in My presence…EVERLASTING LIFE.
I would not leave you without food for your journey…
Your journey home to be with Me forever.

Remember, "Give us this day our daily bread" from My prayer given to you.

COME! Come to the home I prepared for you before the world began!

WORD OF GOD

John 15:10, "If you keep my commandments, you will abide in my love, just as I have kept my Father's commandments and abide in his love."

Matthew 6:11-13, "Give us this day our daily bread; And forgive us our debts, as we also have forgiven our debtors; and lead us not into temptation, but deliver us from evil."

John 6:50-51, "This is the bread which comes down from heaven, that a man may eat of it and not die. I am the living bread which came down from heaven; if anyone eats of this bread, he will live forever; and the bread which I shall give for the life of the world is my flesh."

Revelation 22:17, "The Spirit and the Bride say, 'Come.' And let him who hears say, 'Come.' And let him who is thirsty come, let him who desires take the water of life without price."

What am I personally speaking to you through the photograph, reflection and Scripture? During your day I invite you to continue in My presence, remembering those truths I have revealed to you personally, responding to Me by writing to Me what touched your heart.

*"Light, radiance and grace are in the Trinity and from the Trinity...
We acknowledge the Trinity, holy and perfect,
to consist of the Father, the Son and the Holy Spirit...
It is a wholly creative and energizing reality,
self-consistent and undivided in its active power, for the Father makes all things through the Word and in the Holy Spirit. In this way the unity of the holy Trinity is preserved... Even the gifts that the Spirit dispenses to individuals are given by the Father through the Word.
For all that belongs to the Father belongs also to the Son,
and so the graces given by the Son in the Spirit are true gifts of the Father.
Similarly, when the Spirit dwells in us, the Word who bestows the Spirit is in us too, and the Father is present in the Word.
This is the meaning of the text: My Father and I will come to him and make our home with him. For where the light is, there also is the radiance; and where the radiance is, there too are its power and its resplendent grace."*

Saint Athanasius the Great † A.D. 373

Your 'Yes' Will Become a Resounding 'Yes'!

Beloved, <u>look</u> at the photograph. What draws your interest? <u>Read</u> the reflection and the Scriptures, <u>reflect</u> upon them, linger, <u>rest</u> and be <u>restored</u> in My Truth. <u>Respond</u> with your heart to Me and <u>remain</u> with Me as I remain with you.

My Child,

As much as My cross has encountered your life,
  Do you still not yet see how shallowly it has been planted?
    Though you feel as though it has cost you your life,
      Do you see how much deeper yet it needs to go?

Your "Yes" has to be a continuing "Yes" throughout the day...
  A "Yes" continually until your self-life dies yet more,
    And there is nothing left of it except for your "Yes",
      And then your "Yes" will become a resounding "Yes"
        That is stronger than death...

God's Infinite Design as Creator

Just as it was in the life of My Son.
His "Yes" rang throughout each of every one of His days,
Until His final "Yes" resounded throughout all time.

Oh that you would long for others to know My voice. As a gift from Me,
Through the Holy Spirit, I grant your desire to long all would know My voice.
I give it freely…freely give what has been freely given unto you!

Sheep are lost without knowing the shepherd's voice. His voice is joy.
His voice is comfort, safety, food, water, trust, contentment.
Teach them to know My voice…comfort them,
Pray with them…pray for them.
Freely give what you have been freely given.
Show them My longing fiery love for them!

WORD OF GOD

Hebrews 12:2, "looking to Jesus the pioneer and perfecter of our faith, who for the joy that was set before him endured the cross, despising the shame, and is seated at the right hand of the throne of God."

James 5:12, "But above all, my brethren, do not swear, either by heaven or by earth or with any other oath, but let your yes be yes and your no be no, that you may not fall under condemnation."

Romans 6:6, "We know that our old self was crucified with him so that the sinful body might be destroyed, and we might no longer be enslaved to sin."

Ezekiel 34:12, "As shepherds seek out their flocks when they are among their scattered sheep, so I will seek out my sheep. I will rescue them from all the places to which they have been scattered on a day of clouds and thick darkness."

Matthew 9:36, "When he saw the crowds, he had compassion for them, because they were harassed and helpless, like sheep without a shepherd."

What am I personally speaking to you through the photograph, reflection and Scripture? During your day I invite you to continue in My presence, remembering those truths I have revealed to you personally, responding to Me by writing to Me what touched your heart.

Be Ready for What is Coming

Beloved, <u>look</u> at the photograph. What draws your interest? <u>Read</u> the reflection and the Scriptures, <u>reflect</u> upon them, linger, <u>rest</u> and be <u>restored</u> in My Truth. <u>Respond</u> with your heart to Me and <u>remain</u> with Me as I remain with you.

My Child,

I have waited for you, longed for your coming,
  As a Mother or Father longs for their child.
    Let Me embrace you My child,
      My friend, Lover of My Heart.--

My Child, be ready for what is coming,
  Be ready for My coming,
    Be ready with your heart,
      Be ready with your love,
        Be ready with your life.
          Be prepared,
            Be prepared for My coming

Into this circumstance
Into this situation…
Into this time of difficulty.
Be prepared for a time…
A time of new beginnings!

Finish your work which I have given. Be not distracted! This too will pass…
Always, the distractions posed by the enemy will all pass. This too will pass.

Be still…Be at rest…All have a right to freely choose their own destiny.
There is time for all…as we wait in patience for one another.
All will be fulfilled, as it is given unto Me.
Rest in Me…not in others or in any thing!
I know you are tired. Rest in My arms tonight.
I will comfort you. I long to give you My rest!

WORD OF GOD

Revelation 21:5, "And he who sat upon the throne said, 'Behold, I make all things new." Also he said, "Write this, for these words are trustworthy and true.'"

Matthew 24:44, "Therefore you also must be ready; for the Son of man is coming at an hour you do not expect."

1 Peter 3:15, "But in your hearts reverence Christ as Lord. Always be prepared to make a defense to anyone who calls you to account for the hope that is in you, yet do it with gentleness and reverence;"

Acts 9:31, "Meanwhile the church… had peace and was built up. Living in the fear of the Lord and in the comfort of the Holy Spirit, it increased in numbers."

What am I personally speaking to you through the photograph, reflection and Scripture? During your day I invite you to continue in My presence, remembering those truths I have revealed to you personally, responding to Me by writing to Me what touched your heart.

"A scrap of knowledge about sublime things is worth more than any amount about trivialities."

Saint Thomas Aquinas, Doctor of the Church † 1274

Decide to Live with Me

My Child,

Life is mine to give…Life is mine to take.
　　Life on this earth is but a passing day in My eternal love.
　　　　All life is part of My being…one with Me…
　　　　　　One in My love… or separated from Me.
　　　　　　　　Each one chooses life with Me… or separation from Me,
　　　　　　　　　　According to his own inclinations of heart,
　　　　　　　　　　Decisions of will.

Decide to live with Me…one in Me, and one in My purposes,
　　Which are often different from your own purposes,
　　　　For I love you My child…I love you.
　　　　　　Herald forth My coming again in glory and prepare the way.

Prepare men's hearts, I will show you the way.
Your body is feeling tired and hurting.
You are needing strength.
Let Me strengthen you My child.
Let Me give you hope!
Know that I love you.

I am always with you My child.
I walk before you to draw those to whom I lead you… with My love,
It is My work and not your own. It is My love that does the drawing.
Only take each step…one by one…with Me. I will show to you the way.
I will not ask more of you than you are able to complete.
Take one step at time. My beloved one,
I will give to you the time to do My work of Love.
Trust Me!

WORD OF GOD

1 Timothy 1:15-17, "…Christ Jesus came into the world to save sinners… that in me, as the foremost (sinner), Jesus Christ might display his perfect patience for an example to those who were to believe in him for eternal life. To the King of ages, immortal, invisible the only God, be honor and glory for ever and ever…"

Isaiah 55:9, "For as the heavens are higher than the earth, so are my ways higher than your ways and my thoughts than your thoughts.

Galatians 2:20, "And it is no longer I who live, but it is Christ who lives in me. And the life I now live in the flesh I live by faith in the Son of God, who loved me and gave himself for me."

Ephesians 2:4, "But God, who is rich in mercy, out of the great love with which he loved us, even when we were dead through our trespasses, made us alive…"

What am I personally speaking to you through the photograph, reflection and Scripture? During your day I invite you to continue in My presence, remembering those truths I have revealed to you personally, responding to Me by writing to Me what touched your heart.

"O Lord God almighty... I bless You and glorify You through the eternal and heavenly high priest Jesus Christ, Your beloved Son, through whom be glory to You, with Him and the Holy Spirit, both now and forever."

Saint Polycarp, Disciple of the Apostle John, Early Church Apostolic Father, and Bishop of Smyrna † A.D. 155

My Words

Beloved, <u>look</u> at the photograph. What draws your interest? <u>Read</u> the reflection and the Scriptures, <u>reflect</u> upon them, linger, <u>rest</u> and be <u>restored</u> in My Truth. <u>Respond</u> with your heart to Me and <u>remain</u> with Me as I remain with you.

My Child,

My words are...
   Spoken into your night...
      Spoken into your day...
         Spoken into your grief...
            Spoken into your joy,

My words are…
        Spoken into your future…
            Spoken into your pain…
                Spoken into your past…
                    Spoken into old age,
                        My words are…
                            Spoken into your hurry…
                                Spoken into your fears…
                                    Spoken into your sanctuary through the years.

Recognize Me and My words, in the midst of love…
        Recognize Me in the midst of family strife…
            Recognize Me in the Spring, Fall and Winter of your life…
                Recognize Me in the Quiet…
                    Recognize Me in the Still.

Know the time is now…Know the time is ripe!
        Would I leave you always not knowing what is just out of sight?
            Know that always I have known exactly what is to be…
                Preparing all that is to go on right before you and Me.
                    It is not early…It is not late…it is right on time…Our date!

You are mine and I love you!
        See yourself for who you are in My eyes.
            Have I not called you to live in My Body?
                Don't you know that you are "beautiful" in Spirit in My eyes?
                    Didn't I grace you and have mercy upon you at the beginning?
                        I have a plan for you…sinner though you are.
                            All you need know is that you need Me.
                                Respond to My love towards you that I initiate…
                                    And I will rejoice in you!

Know and believe that I give to you…
        Understanding according to what I ask of you.
            When you give "all" that you have to give…
                You will find that you have more and more to give…
                    As when I multiply the fortunes of those…
                        Who give freely to Me out of their riches.
                            I wish to give to you My life today…
                                That you may live My life…not your own.

As long as you seek to live with your life, your strength…
        You will not find satisfaction. Seek to live with My life…
            And you will find fulfillment. Life in this world…
                Will never "measure up…will never fulfill…

Only life in the world to come will bring fulfillment…
Permanent contentment and peace.

I wish to give to you My new life this day…
A new beginning…a new resting in My love, in My order…
And in the peace that it brings…a new heart…a new mind…
With which to do My will…I love you…
Come with Me… let us run together in life… rejoice!

WORD OF GOD

Deuteronomy 12:28, "Be careful to heed all these words which I command you, that it may go well with you and with your children after you for ever, when you do what is good and right in the sight of the LORD your God."

1 Corinthians 2:13, "And we impart this in words not taught by human wisdom but taught by the Spirit…"

1 Thessalonians 4:18, "Therefore comfort one another with these words."

Mark 8:38, "For whoever is ashamed of me and of my words in this adulterous and sinful generation, of him will the Son of man also be ashamed, when he comes in the glory of his Father with the holy angels."

John 13:7, "Jesus answered, "You do not know now what I am doing, but later you will understand."

Baruch 5:9, "For God will lead… with joy, in the light of his glory, with the mercy and righteousness that come from him."

What am I personally speaking to you through the photograph, reflection and Scripture? During your day I invite you to continue in My presence, remembering those truths I have revealed to you personally, responding to Me by writing to Me what touched your heart.

"There is one God. . . There is a perfect Trinity, in glory and eternity and sovereignty, neither divided nor estranged. Wherefore there is nothing either created or in servitude in the Trinity; nor anything super induced, as if at some former period it was non-existent, and at some later period it was introduced. And thus neither was the Son ever wanting to the Father, nor the Spirit to the Son; but without variation and without change, the same Trinity abides ever." (DECLARATION OF FAITH, A.D. 265).

Saint Gregory the Wonderworker † A.D. 270

God's Infinite Design as Creator

I Love You as I Have Formed You

Beloved, <u>look</u> at the photograph. What draws your interest? <u>Read</u> the reflection and the Scriptures, <u>reflect</u> upon them, linger, <u>rest</u> and be <u>restored</u> in My Truth. <u>Respond</u> with your heart to Me and <u>remain</u> with Me as I remain with you.

Beloved,

I have given you the love you desire to have for My people, My church, as a gift.
It is nothing you have accomplished, nor have understood on your own…
Rather it is My love, given freely as a gift,
For you have asked with a sincere heart.
(Don't forget, with My love comes
The ability to do what needs to be done for others.)

I love you as I have formed you...

Not as you have formed yourself, for you are the work of <u>My</u> hand.

I could have formed you perfectly in your sight,

And in the sight of the world,

But I chose to form you perfectly according to <u>My</u> sight.

Know that I behold you as perfect,

And that I am also in your brothers and sisters.

You are perfect in My sight,

Because of the presence of

My Son and His blood

Over you.

I love you because you are perfect in Him, not perfect of yourself.

I am Spirit, and what I see is your spirit.

What others are to see in you...

Is <u>your spirit, filled with My Spirit</u>!

Know that when you do preparation to serve others,

Even then, while you are doing planning and preparation,

You are "washing the feet", of those you serve, just

As My Son washed the feet of His apostles. Beloved,

Be content knowing even the time doing preparation

Is valued in My eyes...reminding Me

of My much loved Son!

A gift of love is yours to give...pure grace is Mine to give.

This is a time of grace...It is important to pray and ask wholeheartedly...

For this grace... sharing with Me the needs of your heart and others.

My grace is always present...always available...and

I am gracing you at this time to be aware of its flow.

Pray with expectancy and faith!

Today is a new beginning in your love for Me...and in our love together.

Come to Me often and much...you will need this...

As life is about to speed up. It will be your refuge and strength.

Know this is My doing...Be not afraid...nor second guess yourself.

All is in My very capable hands! Follow and you will see...

My times are now!... I go before you...Trust in Me!

Rejoice in Me this day...a day above many others...

Ordained by Me...ordained by My Father...led by the Spirit.

Never are you alone...He has heard your every sigh...

He has heard the cries of your heart and the soul of your grief.

God's Infinite Design as Creator

But too, He has seen His own heart formed in you…
And in others close to you…and He has rejoiced in you!
Oh little one…be encouraged…there is My glory to come.
Rejoice! For I surround you in My love and…dance over you as I
Danced on the day of your salvation… for I Am mighty...
I overcome strongholds… I fill you with My love!

WORD OF GOD

1 Peter 4:10, "As each has received a gift, employ it for one another, as good stewards of God's varied grace:"

Isaiah 64:8, "Yet, O LORD, thou art our Father; we are the clay, and thou art our potter; we are all the work of thy hand."

Act 13:52, "And the disciples were filled with joy and with the Holy Spirit."

Philippians 2:1-4, "If then there is any encouragement in Christ, any consolation from love, any sharing in the Spirit, any compassion and sympathy, make my joy complete: be of the same mind, having the same love, being in full accord and of one mind. Do nothing from selfish ambition or conceit, but in humility regard others as better than yourselves. Let each of you look not to your own interests, but to the interests of others."

Psalm 131:1-2, "O LORD, my heart is not lifted up, my eyes are not raised too high; I do not occupy myself with things too great and too marvelous for me.
But I have calmed and quieted my soul like a weaned child with its mother; my soul is like the weaned child that is with me."

2 Corinthians 10:4-5, "For the weapons of our warfare are not merely human, but they have divine power to destroy strongholds. We destroy arguments and every proud obstacle raised up against the knowledge of God, and we take every thought captive to obey Christ."

What am I personally speaking to you through the photograph, reflection and Scripture? During your day I invite you to continue in My presence, remembering those truths I have revealed to you personally, responding to Me by writing to Me what touched your heart.

It Brings into Being that Which Was Not

"Christ the Saviour (Pantokrator)" Saint Catherine's Monastery, Mount Sinai, 6th century

God's Infinite Design as Creator

My Lord,
I bow before Your will.
I bow before Your Holy Face
That gazes upon me,
That gazes upon the whole world.
I bow before You and I plead Your
Mercy upon me,
And upon all whom I lift to You, oh Lord.
Pour down Your blessings upon each one like a mighty river,
Let Your Holy Name be glorified over the earth,
Oh Lord Jesus Christ!

Beloved,

It will be done according to My will.
    Trust in Me and know that I go with you.
        Truly I am the one who sustains you; who daily brings Life and Joy.

Follow after Me. Seek Me earnestly and
    You will see wonders that are pure gifts from My hand.
        It is I who chooses
            To use,
                To move,
                    To call,
                        To bring into being
                            That which was not.

I see into the depths of men's hearts and into the depth of your heart My child.
    Trust in Me. I love you.
        Know that I am with you.
            Follow Me. Your Lord… Your Lover…Your King.
            Be at peace…Be at rest.
                Yes, move on with what I have asked of you. But
                    At the same time be at peace. Rest in Me. Trust in Me.
                    All will be done…I have allotted you the time.

I have gone before you. All is prepared. It is upon Me…
    It is not upon you. Light and late is the load I have given unto you.
        Rejoice in what is to come. Count it as finished. Held in My hands…
            Held in My heart…flaming with light…
            Hot with the fire of My love!

Colossians 1:9-14, "We have not ceased to pray for you, asking that you may be filled with the knowledge of his will in all spiritual wisdom and understanding, to lead a life worthy of the Lord, fully pleasing to him, bearing fruit in every good work and increasing in the knowledge of God. May you be strengthened with all power according to his glorious might, for all endurance and patience with joy, giving thanks to the Father, who has qualified us to share in the inheritance of the saints in light. He has delivered us from the dominion of darkness and transferred us to the kingdom of his beloved Son, in whom we have redemption, the forgiveness of sins."

Proverbs 8:17, "I love those who love me, and those who seek me diligently find me."

Matthew 17:2, "And he was transfigured before them, and his face shone like the sun, and his garments became white as light."

Revelation 22:4, "They shall see his face, and his name shall be on their forehead."

Hebrews 12:29, "for indeed our God is a consuming fire."

What am I personally speaking to you through the photograph, reflection and Scripture? During your day I invite you to continue in My presence, remembering those truths I have revealed to you personally, responding to Me by writing to Me what touched your heart.

"Since, also, there is but one unbegotten Being,
God, even the Father;
and one only-begotten Son, God, the Word and man;
and one Comforter, the Spirit of truth;
and also one preaching,
and one faith, and
one baptism;"

Saint Ignatius of Antioch † A.D. 107

My Gifts Come with Faithfulness and Perfection of Timing!

Beloved, <u>look</u> at the photograph. What draws your interest? <u>Read</u> the reflection and the Scriptures, <u>reflect</u> upon them, linger, <u>rest</u> and be <u>restored</u> in My Truth. <u>Respond</u> with your heart to Me and <u>remain</u> with Me as I remain with you.

My Child,

Under each and every dream and hope, there are requirements to be met...
  Hardships to be experienced, love to be learned, teachings to be taught...
    Desires to be quenched, and new desires added.

Hope followed by My Father's faithfulness...
  Will always come with My cross, or it is not My gift,
    Always the Holy Spirit gives gifts of Joy
      With faithfulness and perfection of timing,
        Not out of season or without rain...
          Not without pruning or fertilizing,
            Not without weeding or cultivating.

You will come to recognize the signs of the times as you watch for Me My child,
Watch for Me! I am with you. Lo I am with you unto the end of the age
And for ages to come. Look for Me in your day to lead your way.
I go before you to prepare a place for you in My glory.
I will never abandon you or forsake you. I am with you always!

My prayer, Oh Father,
is that in Your great mercy and kindness
You will meet me in my weakness and pour forth
Your grace upon me to accomplish what You wish to do;
that Your divine plan in my life,
in my family's life, and in the world will be brought about,
for I see now Lord who You are and who I am not!
I see Your mercy
and the humility of Your love and kingship,
and I seek to be under Your authority and not my own.

My Child,

I accept you as My servant My Beloved One,
For I know who you are…and who you are not and
My heart burns with longing to bless you.
I see your sin and I have given you power…
In the blood of the Cross to overcome it.
I accept you washed clean by the blood of My Son,
And empowered by the Holy Spirit to serve.
There is still so much more to come Beloved One!

WORD OF GOD

1 Peter 2:24, "He himself bore our sins in his body on the tree, that we might die to sin and live to righteousness. By his wounds you have been healed."

Acts 13:52, "And the disciples were filled with joy and with the Holy Spirit."

John 14:1-2, "Let not your hearts be troubled; believe in God, believe in me also. In my Father's house are many rooms; if it were not so, would I have told you that I go to prepare a place for you?"

John 15:1-5, "I am the true vine, and my Father is the vinedresser. Every branch of mine that bears no fruit, he takes away, and every branch that does bear fruit he prunes, that it may bear more fruit. You are already made clean by the word which I have spoken to you. Abide in me, and I in you. As the branch cannot bear fruit by itself, unless it abides in the vine, neither can you, unless you abide in me. I am the vine, you are the branches. He who abides in me, and I in him, he it is that bears much fruit."

What am I personally speaking to you through the photograph, reflection and Scripture? During your day I invite you to continue in My presence, remembering those truths I have revealed to you personally, responding to Me by writing to Me what touched your heart.

"I knew more distinctly than ever before
the Three Divine Persons, the Father, the Son, and the Holy Spirit.
But their being, their equality, and their majesty are one.
My soul is in communion with these Three; but I do not know how to express
this in words; yet my soul understands this well.
Whoever is united to One of the Three Persons is thereby united
to the whole Blessed Trinity, for this Oneness is indivisible."

Saint Maria Faustina † 1938

"The Church, though dispersed throughout the whole world, even to the
ends of the earth, has received from the apostles and their disciples this faith:…
one God, the Father Almighty, Maker of heaven, and earth, and the sea,
and all things that are in them; and in one Christ Jesus, the Son of God,
who became incarnate for our salvation; and in the Holy Spirit, who
proclaimed through the prophets the dispensations of God,
and the advents, and the birth from a virgin, and the passion, and the
resurrection from the dead, and the ascension into heaven in the flesh of
the beloved Christ Jesus, our Lord."

Saint Irenaeus, Early Church Father, Bishop of Lyons † A.D. 190
As a boy he listened to Polycarp, the disciple of John.

THE LONGING, FIERY LOVE OF THE HOLY TRINITY   123

Surrender to God's Divine Will

Most Holy Trinity, Godhead indivisible,
FATHER, SON, AND HOLY SPIRIT,
my first beginning and my last end,
You have made me in accord with Your own image
and likeness.

Grant that all the thoughts of my mind
all the words of my tongue,
all the affections of my heart,
and all the actions of my being
may always be conformed to Your holy will.

So may I, having seen You veiled in appearance
here below by means of faith, come at last
to contemplate You face to face,
in the perfect possession of You forever in heaven.
Amen.

Consecration to the Holy Trinity

I vow and consecrate to God all that is in me:
my memory and my action to GOD THE FATHER;
my understanding and my words to GOD THE SON;
my will and my thoughts to GOD THE HOLY SPIRIT.

I consecrate my heart and my body, my tongue, my senses
And all my sorrows to SACRED HUMANITY OF JESUS CHRIST,
who consented to be betrayed into the hands of men
And to suffer the torment of the cross for me.
Amen.

Saint Francis De Sales † 1622

Your Name: _____   Date: _____

THE LONGING, FIERY LOVE OF THE HOLY TRINITY

SAINT QUOTES

Valid Baptism Only in the the Most Holy Trinity

"He [Jesus] commanded them to baptize the Gentiles in the name of the Father and of the Son and of the Holy Spirit. How then do some say that though a Gentile be baptized… never mind how or of whom, so long as it be done in the name of Jesus Christ, the remission of sins can follow – when Christ himself commands the nations to be baptized in the full and united Trinity?" (LETTERS 73:18).

Saint Cyprian of Carthage † A.D. 253

LITURGICAL SEASONS
For the Series <u>God's Burning Love</u>

Months	Liturgical Season	Volume
DECEMBER JANUARY	Advent and Christmastide	**Volume 1** The Tender Love of Jesus Aflame for You
FEBRUARY MARCH	Lenten Season	**Volume 2** The Burning Love of Jesus Given for You
APRIL MAY	Eastertide and Mary's Month	**Volume 3** The Mothering Heart of God Through Mary
JUNE JULY	Ascensiontide and Pentecost	**Volume 4** The Holy Spirit's Blazing Love for You
		Volume 5 The Longing, Fiery Love of the Holy Trinity for You
AUGUST SEPTEMBER	Ordinary Time	**Volume 6** The Father's Beautiful Love for You
OCTOBER NOVEMBER	The Month of All Souls and All Saints, Living and Deceased	**Volume 7** The Mercy Gate: Intercessions

Made in the USA
Columbia, SC
10 December 2021

50789711R10071